Progress, Stability &

Hope

African Americans and the Marriage Option

Rev. Dr. Roosevelt Walker, Sr.

Walker With You, LLC
Nashville, Tennessee

Progress, Stability & Hope
African Americans and The Marriage Option

Copyright 2022 by Rev. Dr. Roosevelt Walker, Sr.
Published by Walker With You, LLC
Trade Paperback ISBN 979-8-9874572-0-7
Ebook - ISBN 979-8-9874572-1-4
Printed in the United States of America

For information contact:
Rev. Dr. Roosevelt Walker, Sr.
Email: walkerwithyoullc1@gmail.com

Scripture quotations, unless otherwise noted, are from the Holy Bible, Christian Standard Bible (CSB) Version. Copyright 2017 by Holman Bible Publishers. Nashville, Tennessee.

Editors: Janice M. Allen janiceallen7519@gmail.com
J. L. Campbell jlcampbellwrites@gmail.com
Cover design by J.L. Woodson for Woodson Creative Studio
Interior design by Lissa Woodson for Woodson Creative Studio

Table of Contents

♦ ACKNOWLEDGEMENTS ♦

My gratitude extends across a handful of special individuals. I need to first praise and thank God in Christ. What can I say? Other than, you are my Lord, Leader, and Savior. Thank you, Jesus. I love you more than I can say.

To my wife, Benita, who this book is dedicated to, and who I have affectionately called BJ for thirty-four years now. Sweetie, thank you. Your strength, support, love, and faith are what marriage is all about.

To Rev. Dr. Terry Wardle, Dr. Anne M. Halley, and others, what an all-star line-up of pros and practitioners that led the way in helping to form, shape, and inspire my understanding of the art, science, and Spirit behind Formational Counseling. Thank you all.

I also owe a debt of gratitude to each of the individuals and couples who journeyed under my tutelage, by way of the Holy Spirit through a Formational Counseling marital small group experience. I pray your marriage was made stronger as a result.

As well I extend a big round of applause to a gifted team of literary editors, graphic designers, etc., especially Janice Allen, who helped bring this book to fruition.

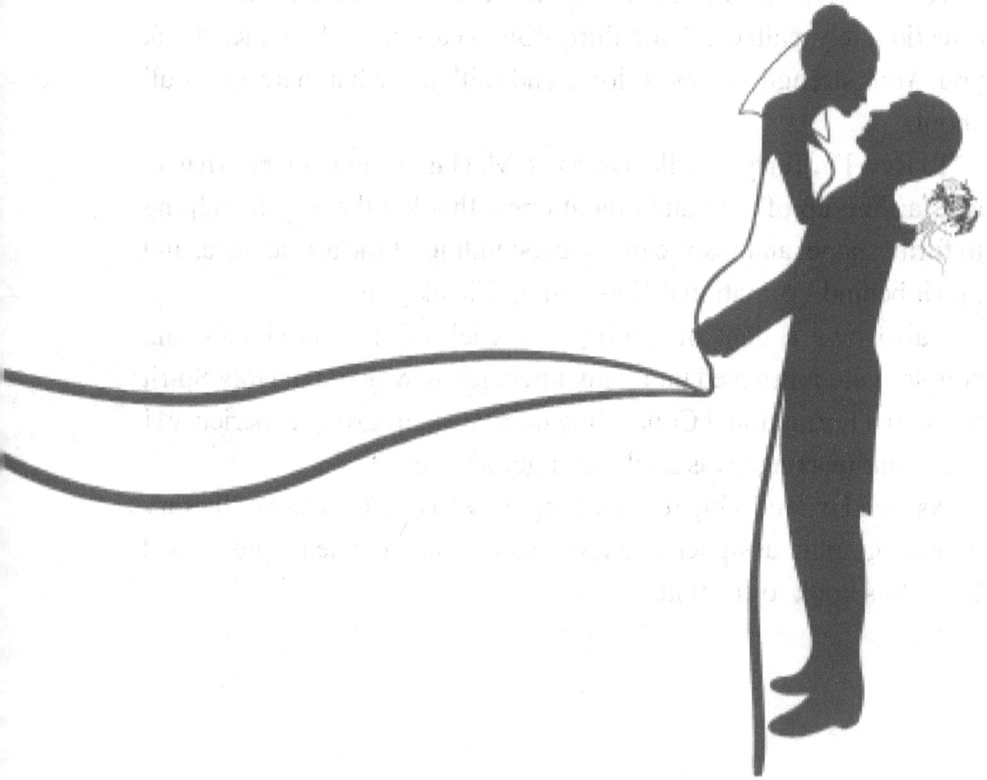

[illegible]

[illegible]
[illegible]
[illegible]
[illegible]

[illegible]
[illegible]
[illegible]
[illegible]
[illegible]
[illegible]
[illegible]
[illegible]
[illegible]

Introduction

A wedding is an event. A marriage is an experience.

Every wedding is a one-and-done deal. The celebration of the exchanging of vows between a man and a woman is over in a matter of hours. In contrast, a marriage involves those two people endeavoring to live life together not for a few hours, but until death do them part.

I'm married to a wonderful woman who is African American like me. Our marriage of thirty-four years has survived and thrived despite challenging obstacles. But that wouldn't have been possible had we not discovered and fully embraced one critical relational reality: no marriage can flourish unless the couple undertakes the struggle to keep the marriage option alive. This means both individuals each day, guided by Jesus Christ, make the choice to stay in and sustain the relationship through any and every struggle, with the goal of succeeding in marriage.

Sadly, since the mid-1960s, marriage in the U.S., particularly in the African American community, has become less of an option and more like an obstacle to cultivating fulfilling male and female relations. Take for instance the example of a husband and wife named Susan and Joe in Nancy Boyd-Franklin's classic work, *Black Families in Therapy: A Multi-systems Approach.*

A young black couple in their early 30s, Susan and Joe had one child. Joe was a lawyer and Susan had been a teacher prior to the birth of their son. They sought counseling after Joe hit Susan. She reported that verbal abuse had been a problem for more than three years, but this was the first time Joe struck her. The source of his agony: after finishing law school in three years, Joe had been unable to pass the bar exam. Each year as the time for the bar approached, he became angry and verbally abusive.

In counseling, Joe denied and minimized the problem. He even threatened to withdraw from treatment. The therapist saw him alone for a session to help him explore his feelings about the exam—the rage it evoked in him, and his fears of failure. Joe was then able to share these feelings with his wife. He revealed that because he feared she would condemn him for his failure, he criticized her constantly about her own insecurities. Whenever she asserted herself, he became enraged, accused her of not caring about him, and threatened to hit her. Both partners had hidden their difficulties from extended family, friends, and neighbors. They kept up the "perfect couple" façade at church, around his work colleagues, and even at family gatherings. The therapist worked with them for many months before they were finally able to stop minimizing their issues, confront their fears, and begin to ask for support from each other.[1]

All kinds of personal and interpersonal issues plagued Susan and Joe, both as individuals and as a couple. This husband and wife demonstrate two types of resistance that is common in black couples wrestling to commit to or succeed in holy matrimony.

The first, as Nancy Boyd-Franklin points out in her book, is a resistance to counseling.[2] This is when the husband, wife, or both are reluctant to seek help from professional, pastoral, or lay counseling when issues threaten to make the union self-destruct. Yet in Proverbs 11:14 and 15:22, the Bible advocates that "in the abundance of counsel there is safety and victory."

The second form of resistance, chiefly germane to our focus, exposes an even graver condition often prevalent in blacks who are married or contemplating marriage. It is a spoken or unspoken resistance to understanding and accepting the need to undertake "the struggle for progress" in all the right ways to help keep the marriage option alive. In biblical terms it might be said like this: married or engaged black men and women should understand the importance and accept the need to "fight the good fight of faith" through Christ to salvage and succeed in their marriage.

Moving from One Angst to Another

It's no secret that the African American community has had a tumultuous and often horrifying journey in their quest to be fully embraced as American citizens. This even applied to marriage. Although marriage has been around for thousands of years, Blacks in America have only been allowed to exercise this right for the last 150 years or so, even though we have been in America for 400 years. For a full two-thirds of that time, or for the first 250 years of the black community's existence in America, legal marriage rights and relations didn't exist.

It's been said that "anything worth having is worth fighting for." Between 1865 and 1965, that proved true concerning black marriage. A marriage between a man and a woman is worth the necessary struggle, or may I say the "sacred struggle," if they wish to experience the unique relational beauty found in a healthy marriage. However, African Americans in large measure seem to be losing the will to fight to keep their marriage option alive. But that was not always the case.

Chapter 1

Black Men and Women Struggle to Gain the Marriage Option

Between 1865 and 1965, our African American ancestors embraced the struggle to fully assert their God-given right in Christ to enjoy love as it was meant to be fully expressed in marriage. As mentioned, from 1965 to the present, the African American community's effort to keep their marriage option alive has undergone serious decline. But prior to 1965, the typical African American man and woman exhibited the ego strength, God-fearing propensity, fortitude of character, and will that helped the community secure the marital rights denied them for centuries. How did such gain come about? It was a struggle!

Before the Civil War, enslaved men and women jumped over a broomstick as a gesture of their respect for the institution of marriage. It signified the spiritual, emotional, and relational bond of the union. However, broom jumping could never certify legal marriage status for slaves. For post-Civil War marriage of ex-slaves to be formalized by the proper authorities and recognized by society, it took the strategic efforts of the U.S. Freedmen's Bureau and the black church, along with the individual moral choice and conviction of the ex-slave community.

How The U.S. Freedmen's Bureau Impacted the Black Marital Option

After the Civil War, millions of America's residents in the South, displaced Blacks and poor Whites alike were hungry, homeless, destitute, and desperate for help with their basic needs. As if that were not enough angst, those Black men and women freed from slavery found themselves nowhere near free from systemic racism and oppression. Enter the Freedmen's Bureau. Author Joyce Hansen says, "The Freedmen's Bureau was the only safety net to keep the emancipated people from falling back into new forms of slavery."[3]

Established by an Act of Congress in March of 1865, the Freedmen's Bureau addressed ten basic needs of ex-slaves. The need for:

1. Food.

2. Shelter.

3. Clothing.

4. Hospitals.

5. Schools.

6. Jobs.

7. Abandoned lands.

8. Conflict mediation.

9. Protection.

10. Marriage.

Did you notice the last need mentioned? *Marriage.* The Freedmen's Bureau was granted congressional civil authority to perform weddings and grant legal marital status to ex-slaves. Thousands of ex-slaves flocked to Freedmen's Bureau offices throughout the South to solemnize their prior "jump the broom" unions, or to legally marry off the engaged. Once the Black couple located and travelled to a Freedmen's Bureau office, its officer or chaplain legalized their nuptials by registering their names into an official ledger or issuing a marriage license or certificate. In her work *The Reconstruction Era,* Betty Stroud remarks that "after emancipation many black couples were eager to legalize their 'slave marriages' thus mass wedding ceremonies involving as many as seventy couples at a time took place at Freedmen's Bureau offices."[4]

To help put in perspective what ex-slave men and women in post-Civil War America had to weather just to formalize their marriage vows, it would help to contrast that to what it takes to secure a marriage license in the twenty-first century.

First, understand that back then, "many local jurisdictions throughout the South demanded high fees to discourage ex-slaves from marrying or simply refused to give them access to courts and licenses."[5] This was because many White southerners saw Black marriage as an affront to the mainstream social order and structure of the times.

Second, the South was a scene of a hostile, humiliating, and protracted Northern (Yankee) Army siege prior to the end of the Civil War. Immediately after the South lost the war, emancipated Blacks faced scorn, rage, and resentment from angry, defeated Southerners called Rebels. Nevertheless, ex-slaves hoping to get married at

Freedmen's Bureau offices travelled considerable distances on foot with puny resources, facing constant danger from post-slavery Rebels.

Ex-slaves endured all this because, as Nora Lee Frankel observed, "being able to create and maintain family ties, anchored in legal marriage, was a crucial element of freedom for former slaves."[6] As slaves, they had not been allowed to enjoy the Judeo-Christian benefit of the traditional family given the laws of the time and the constant threat of separation. But starting in 1865, for the first time since Blacks arrived in America in 1619, the marriage of Black men and women was recognized by law—not just by love.

When my wife and I married in 1988, and when our sons got married some eight to nine years ago, no one—black or white—opposed our union with open, hostile rebellion. We didn't have to secure a slave master's consent, only that of our Heavenly Master. We were not concerned with being confronted by corrupt so-called protectors like Klansmen and others on the route to a U.S. Freedman's Bureau office to have the Walker names recorded and recognized as husband and wife. Recognized not only in the Lord's and our love's eyes, but also in the legal view of society. The county clerk gladly provided us a paper license in exchange for that green paper we used to pay the required fee. The fact that our ancestors endured horrific treatment to earn the right of legal marriage recognition for themselves, and for their progeny, deserves our utmost respect. Oh, how it deepens my devotion to God in Christ for using them in this way.

How the Black Church Impacted the Black Marriage Option

The black church, anchored by its belief in Jesus, was a source of sustained impetus and communal thrust in legitimizing Black marriage. For centuries, the Black church has been central to the African American community's survival and success, both before and after the Civil War. The Black church (or as it used to be called, the Negro church), has been to Blacks in America what a womb is to an unborn child: *incubation for growth and development.* Lincoln and Mamiya characterized its pervasive influence by saying "the black church has no challenger as the cultural womb of the black community. Not only did it give birth to new institutions such as schools, banks, insurance companies, and low-income housing, but it also provided an academy and an arena for political activities, and it nurtured young talent for musical, dramatic, and artistic development."[7] Post-slavery, the Black church began aggressively advancing the cause of the legal option to marry by "encouraging ex-slaves to build strong families by marrying and staying with one spouse—and to remain faithful to that spouse and their children."[8] In doing so, Black preachers helped do what White missionaries or preachers could not: build a strong Black marriage *ethic* among ex-slaves. This effort resulted not only in strong Black marriages, but strong Black families too. In turn, this helped build strong, robust African American communities, not simply strong Black churches, throughout America. Black churches and their preachers did not stop at advocating for the legal marriage option among ex-slaves. They aggressively enforced it within the ranks of the Black church community. All over the South after the Civil War, Black churches adopted policy stipulating that cohabitating adults would be denied church membership unless they could produce proof of marriage.[9]

The Black church oversight stood in complete contrast to some of the slave behavior previously sanctioned by their masters. "Slave masters dispensed with even informal slave marriages, refusing to allow men and women to live as a couple. On some plantations, likely many given the business profit motive, it was common to find women who had borne children by four or five different fathers. The man may have as many women as he wishes, wrote an observer on one such farm or plantation, and the women as many men."[10] E. Franklin Frazier, author of *The Negro Church in America*, notes that the removal of the authority of masters as the result of the Civil War and Emancipation caused promiscuous sexual relations to become widespread and permitted the constant changing of spouses. This predicament helped catapult the Black church into the forefront as the Black community's premier spiritual and social-moral agency. The Black church "became and have remained until recently (circa 1965 or so), the most important agency of social control among Negroes. The churches undertook as organizations to censure unconventional and immoral sex behavior and to punish by expulsion sex offenders and those who violated the monogamous mores."[11] In short, the black church applied its spiritual muscle and moral grit to help correct ungodly sexual practices after Emancipation. This sacred conviction was based on Christ-centered, Bible-informed, spiritually invigorating, and practically lived out principles regarding holy matrimony. Like me, these ancestors believed that "marriage is honorable for all, the marriage bed undefiled and that fornicators and adulterers God will judge," according to Hebrews 13:4 in the Bible.

You're probably wondering how the Black church could get away with such strict governance of marriage and sexual behavior.

The Black church was the "it" agency for social control among ex-slaves and the evolving Black community. Mind you, the Black church, especially the Black ministers who led them, were not totally dictatorial in their role. Rather, they were dominant and not dormant in social and spiritual influence.

How much pushback was there from the black community? Frankel noted that "many freed people marrying after the Civil War sought out a church with an African American congregation and preacher."[12] A Black couple seeking a Black church where there was a Black clergy meant a Black marriage was to take place. One Freedmen's Bureau official wrote in 1865, "freed people all manifest a disposition to marry in the church and prefer a minister of the Gospel to unite them."[13] Ex-slaves wanted and needed to legalize and celebrate their nuptials without degradation in a space where they felt wanted. The Black church was that place. As Frankel and a Freedmen's Bureau official affirm, of utmost importance to most Black adults and the Black church then was clearly an ironclad credence to four life-changing forces: *God in Christ. God's Gospel. God's Gospel Minister. Good moral high ground.*

I find it ironic yet inspiring that what the White-controlled State government, Federal government, mainstream culture, and particularly the White church would not allow for 250 years, the Black church brought to pass: *marriage solidarity* for ex-slaves. No other post-slavery organization or organizational leader, be it the White church and their missionaries, the Freedmen's Bureau and their mainly White-led staff, or former slaveholders themselves, could help reverse the contagion of immorality in Blacks like the Black church and its leader—the Black male minister.

How Individual Moral Choice Impacted
the Black Marriage Option

What shouldn't be understated is the individualized moral willfulness of ex-slaves that helped them earn and elevate legal marriage in their community. I would venture to say that individual moral choice of Black men and women desiring the full blessing of married life eclipsed even the efforts of the U.S. Freedman's Bureau and the Black church as it concerns marriage regulation in the ex-slave community.

The morality of ex-slaves as Christian men and women was expressed in their fight to do their part to secure what was always rightfully theirs—the marriage option. They fought by taking those long, dangerous walks to faraway Freedman's Bureau offices. In a now freed world for the ex-slave hardly anyone could make them do that. However, I believe, an individually held and shared moral ethic, stemming from a cemented Christian moral code within them, did. It took not only ego strength but moral tenacity to do the honorable thing and walk down the aisle to get married. They had to capitalize on their moral ethic to combat the enormous resistance of White Southerners. New federal laws called for Whites to afford their ex-slaves' legal marriage without interference. But as you might imagine, it didn't happen smoothly. Nevertheless, the raw sentiments of Southern sympathizers could not deter the ex-slaves' fervor to vie for legal marriage recognition.

Moral choice impacted the marital longevity of ex-slaves. Records reveal that ex-slave marriages not only survived—but thrived—as marriages are meant by God in Christ to do. Even if we factored in the notion that these ex-slave men and women married solely for financial purposes, partnering to provide a monetary pouch from which they could subsist on, of which the literature indicates was largely not true, it's still a notable feat. To put ex-slaves' marital longevity in perspective, consider the tenure of modern-day marriages. The average length of the modern-day African American marriage is eight and a half years according to a 2009 U.S. Census Bureau report on marriage.[14] In *Slavery Remembered: A Record of Twentieth-Century Slave Narratives,* Paul Escott reports that the average ex-slave marriage lasted forty-four and a half years. This represents a thirty-six year difference between the average length of our formerly enslaved ancestors' marriages and modern-day black marriages. Additionally, Escott reminds us that "almost ninety percent of the former slaves had been married only once or twice, and fewer than nine percent reported three, four, or more marriages. Rarely did broken marriages result from incompatibility of the partners or the irresponsibility, immorality, or desertion of a spouse. The predominant cause of separation was death—not divorce or desertion."[15] In other words, Escott suggests that most ex-slave marriages ended, as God intends for any marriage between a man and woman to end, by death not a divorce certificate.

That said, we need to take a glance at how Black marriage arrived at its current state. I believe it is also necessary to acknowledge that marriages do fail for a variety of reasons. Some people and couples simply do not take advantage of such a sacred relational option, as they should for many reasons. It would be naïve for anyone to think differently. Even ex-slave marriages, while evidently not in large numbers, failed. If we are honest, often the rationale for the failures of modern-day marriages is consistent with

God-given biblical grounds for termination. Biblical grounds like adultery (affairs), spousal abuse, lack of spousal support, religious (faith) incompatibility, or death. Though painful, biblical grounds are not viewed by God in Christ, especially if you are a Christ-follower, as a biblical guarantee for divorce. Nor do they have to be seen that way by you. Right now, however, it seems to me the obvious question the God of the Bible would want us to ask ourselves as people of color is this: *How in the heck are we now grappling with this sullied reality of the Black marriage option after experiencing such a successful history to secure the same?*

Chapter 2

Black Men and Women Strain to Retain the Marriage Option

"Rates of marriage for other groups are higher than rates for African Americans. African Americans also tend to report lower marital satisfaction. As well, African Americans tend to think about divorce more than do Whites and Latinos."[16]

Alarming, isn't it? These findings are from a University of Georgia researcher/professor's study on African Americans and marriage. Equally discouraging is the fact that blacks do not only think about divorce more than other groups nowadays, but act on it more consistently. Stanford law professor and social commentator, Ralph Richard Banks, notes that roughly sixty-six percent of Black marriages compared to fifty percent of White marriages end in divorce. He also found that fifty percent of Black couples divorce within the first ten years of their marriage while less than thirty-three percent of White couples divorce over the same period.[17]

Many factors combine to either stoke or stifle the Black marriage option. One set of them is known as core longings. Core longings is not a phrase we often hear. A simpler label for this term might be inner needs. Dr. Anne Medaglia Halley defines core longings as "the human design by God to feel, desire, and experience an inner and abiding sense of belonging, love, purpose, security, significance, and understanding."[18] By belonging, it's meant to feel, desire, experience and enjoy deep connection leading to a shared relational identity like marriage. Bonding like say a properly fitted hand & glove that produces a warmth that envelopes a couple. By love, it's meant unconditional love. The kind of love, embodied in marriage, that doesn't "keep a record of wrongs, or insist on its own way. Love that is patient, kind, non-envious, not boastful, rude, or self-seeking. Finds no joy in wrong but rejoices in the truth. It bears, believes, is hopeful, and enduring in all things. And never ends" (1 Corinthian 13:4-8). By purpose, it's meant not meandering in marriage with little to no regard for individual and relational usefulness now or for the future. Which would cast shade on the secure nature of the relationship and the people in it. Thus, by security it's meant the repeated messages expressed in various but necessary ways that results in a person being made safe and secure, in every possible way, by and in the relationship. This security is further cemented by a constant reinforcement of personal worth called significance. A significance described as individuals being viewed and handled as valued, unique, and special by God first, and second by their spouse. With understanding, it's meant being able to feel understood. Not just heard or seen in one's exchange of facts, ideas, cliches, input, or feelings but ultimately understood. In Bible terms, this means relationally "in all thy getting, get understanding" (Proverbs 4:7). Or husbands, "dwell with your wives according to understanding" (1 Peter 3:7) of their needs, etc. The same is true for wives. "The absence of these create intolerable longings or what are known as core-longing deficits."[19]

The Primary Core Longings of Black Couples in Marriage

It would be easy to attribute all core-longing deficits that Black men and women experience in matrimony to the absence of love. However, multiple external stressors contribute to the presence of a lot of pain and problems (core-longing deficits) in many Black couples. One thinker on Black marriage identifies them as financial strain, work/occupational status, duties/obligations to extended family, and the presence of children. More often they do not cause core-longing deficits but worsen pre-existing problems concerning "racial/ethnic identity, religiosity, spouse partner/support, social networks, problem solving, mastery and control (and especially pertinent to our conversation on core longings), emotional distress/ negative emotions."[20]. These stressors are not exclusive to Black couples. However, what tends to be more unique to blacks are the stressors of racial discrimination and minority status.[21]

Robert Staples and others argue that the marital mix between Black men and women, unlike their White counterparts, has been decimated by socio-psychological factors that arose partly because of slavery in North America. As he points out, the White family "was a patriarchy sustained by the economic dependence of the female." In contrast, "the system of slavery did not permit the Black male to assume the superordinate role in the family" because "the female was not economically dependent on him," but on the slave master. As Staples points out, the "economic compulsion to marry and remain married" was not present in slave and ex-slave relationships and marriages.[22]

In some ways, it mirrors the effect it has among Black men and women today. However, a few differences are quite notable. For one, the notion of role and economic parity between engaged or married Black men and women has been upended by the explosive growth in the education and economic independence of Black women in America. The Black male-female ratio in college flipped between the time I started college in 1983 and the time I completed my doctoral studies in 2015. As Staples cites, the impact on the socio-psychological relations between Black men and women is real, sometimes even raw and explosive when mishandled.

Any notion of the Black male breadwinner and head of the household has sharply evaporated between 1983 and now. I, along with many Christian Black men and women, believe in the biblical directive found in Ephesians 5:22-23, which tells wives to submit to their husbands, for he is the head of the wife as Christ is the head of the church. But even when the Black sexes attempt to reconcile these education and economic realities to the biblical admonition, it can and does still pose unique relational challenges.

Counselor Audrey B. Chapman in her article, *"The Black Search for Love and Devotion: Facing The Future Against All Odds,"* argues that much of the modern day disconnect that exists between black men and women, and the subsequent disengagement in marriage or for marriage, has to do with many self-effacing stereotypes imposed on both genders.[23] "Black women are called sapphires after the forceful character on the old *Amos and Andy* radio and television shows, and described as controlling, castrating shrews. Black men are told they are unreliable, irresponsible cads, loving and leaving women who make great sacrifices for them."[24] Held broadly, this means that Black men are erratic, lazy, or "worthless" and that Black women who are perceived as hostile or controlling are calculating and uncaring or "unloving." Yet both worth and love are necessary core longings. Such misery is the case with some individuals in all people groups in America and the world. However, such labeling has long tended to be applied to Blacks in America far more than folk in general.

This targeted and wrongly applied labeling continues to be destructive to the unified and individual psyche of Black men and women. Chapman says:

> African Americans who continue to face enormous economic and social disparities are also affected 'emotionally' by their marginal status in this country. Couples may come to me [Audrey] fighting about money, intimacy, communication, and other typical relationship concerns. But invariably I find that the real struggles are internal, with one or both individuals feeling a lack of personal control, a sense of emotional deprivation, a need for nurturance, or a strong sense of helplessness.[25]

The leftover and unresolved issues stemming from such negative labeling by society or self leaves many among the African American sexes feeling and thinking badly of themselves as individuals and spouses. Or, just as bad, thinking badly of the opposite sex. This devalues marriage from the inside-out in the hearts and minds of Blacks everywhere. The late Rev. David A. Seamands says that many individuals come into marriage already indebted—not financially but emotionally. His reasoning is true of Blacks and non-Blacks. He contends that:

> Many married people fail to allow God to do for them what only God can do. Then they ask other human beings, their spouses to do what they cannot possibly do. If they work at it, men make good husbands, and women make good wives. But they make lousy gods. They are not meant for that. And all those wonderful promises people make on their wedding day—I promise to love, care for you, cherish you, through all the circumstances and vicissitudes of life—these are possible only when a heart is secure in God's love, grace, and care. What the person often really means when he says those beautiful words is, I have a lot of terrific inner needs and inner emptiness and debts to pay and I'm going to give you a marvelous opportunity to fill my Grand Canyon and take care of me. Aren't I wonderful?[26]

Many Black people are unaware of possessing such "Grand Canyon-like" inner needs, feelings, beliefs and behaviors, no matter from where they stem. And Black spouses and couples, like others, are often dismissive of the grace, love and caregiving opportunity offered by God in Christ to address such core-longing deficits.

On top of that, another troubling notion has been tracking and dogging Black male and female relations in recent years. That is, Blacks "have assumed a yo-yo or approach-avoidant mentality regarding relationships and focus less on intimacy and more on superficialities" both in and outside of marriage.[27] One ministry leader observes the following about people who behave in this manner:

> In effect, they shut the gates when they should let others in; these leaders (or others) withdraw under pressure. Early family-of-origin experiences may lie at the root of the avoidant reaction. They may have had some experience of psychological pain that taught them an unfortunate lesson: *keep others out.* Avoidants are very hard to help because they keep people, even those who want to help them, at a distance.[28]

Today, unlike in previous generations, especially among slave and ex-slave generations, there seems to exist a generalized pursue-distance phenomenon in male-female relations in America. And this phenomenon appears to be far more widespread and warped among Black men and women relations. Rev. Dr. Terry Wardle would argue it's a breeding ground for all kinds of dysfunctional behavior, emotional upheaval, and false beliefs in marriage. His concept of the structures of healing is defined below:

> Both a caregiver and a care-receiver should think of the structures of inner healing as being like the layers of an onion that color a person's painful predicament. The layers consist or involve the person's life situation,

accompanying dysfunctional behaviors, emotional upheaval, lies and distortions and wounds.[29]

Like the Black married couple illustrated in an earlier section, Black couples combat and may be perplexed by an array of core-longing deficits in their internal and interpersonal make-up and movements as individuals and spouses. Now we'll single out the most common core-longing deficit(s) that tend to dominate Black men and women who are married or engaged.

The Primary Core Longing(s) of Black Men in Marriage

Numerous studies backed-up by U. S. Census data of the last few decades report the excruciating impact of slavery, post-slavery, racism, high unemployment, underemployment, incarceration, fatherlessness, crime against one another, and circumstantial events on the black male psyche. In *What Mama Couldn't Tell Us About Love*, Brenda Richardson and Brenda Wade cite the reasoning of noted psychologist and professor, Nancy Boyd-Franklin as she commented on racism and its impact on Blacks.

> It is difficult to convey fully to someone who has not experienced the insidious, pervasive, and constant impact that racism and discrimination have on the lives of black people in America today. Both affect a black person from birth to death and have an impact on every aspect of family life, from child-rearing practices, courtship, *marriage*, to male-female roles, self-esteem, and cultural and racial identification. They also influence

the way in which black people relate to each other and to the outside world.[30]

Anne Medaglia Halley might even assert that racism can influence how Black couples might attempt to fill each other's core longings. And when it comes to today's typical engaged or married black men, findings strongly pinpoint their primary core longing to be an abiding sense of belonging. Subsequently, if he feels he doesn't belong, he's sure he's being rejected.

Imagine the Black male asking within and without: Do I belong in this corporation, job, or country? Or worse, do I belong in jail? Do I belong in the family I grew up in, meaning, was I born or adopted into it? Do I belong as a father? Do I belong to my real self or some alter ego? Do I belong in this marriage to this Black woman? Most critically do I belong to God in Christ?

All of these have huge ramifications for marriage. Understandably, if one feels he does not belong, it will be difficult, perhaps even impossible, to give or receive the other core longings of love, purpose, security, significance, and understanding. All six core longings are vital for Black men and women. But belonging is extremely significant, relative to the Black male experience. According to one theologian, the feelings of rejection in a man who has a bankrupt sense of belonging can and do manifest in destructive ways[31]. This "unhealed rejection becomes seedbeds of … bitterness, envy, rage, fear of rejection and a sense of inferiority."[32] These noxious emotions are quite common to the Black male experience. They haunted our Black male and female ancestors during and after slavery, and still rage within Black males and females today, resonating as an issue of belonging in the black male.

Rejection often manifests more intensely in the black male psyche and day-to-day experience than in others. For many African American husbands, and single men soon to be married, unhealed rejection is experienced as "neglect, disloyalty, betrayal, unfairness, mockery and physical abuse"[33] just looking for a place to let go or let fly. Unfortunately, that place is often found in a wife or fiancée. This relational toxicity is bad for the father and mother support systems of Black children. One thing that can really fan the flames is the male's employment status.

Men feel more like men when they are gainfully working. But the incidence of black male unemployment as a negative result of slavery and racism in America leaves black fathers feeling less paternal and more prone to abandon their wives and families to be single.[34] Such fatherly acts of apostasy have the tendency to poison core longings in and between Black men, women, and children. Ken Canfield, former president of the National Center for Fathering, forcefully asserts that kids need their fathers. I could not agree more. Most reasonable people would also agree. He emphasizes that "kids need us (fathers) to claim them as our own."[35] In a word, kids need to know, feel, and think they belong. He also says, "telling children 'you are mine' and telling the world 'they are mine' is the first stage of a father's [and mother's] commitment. Such expressions of commitment give a child a sense of belonging and connectedness."[36] This is something many adult Black men and women currently in or contemplating marriage did not receive as kids.

The core longing implications are huge for these men and women in marriage. Moreover, Blacks would do well to keep in mind that "there are no statistics to indicate how many more of us (Blacks) had parents who lived with us but were so caught up in the complexities of their own struggles that they left us [speaking specifically here about black male and female children who are now adults] feeling unsupported."[37] Or left these adults harboring core-longing deficits for which they are expected to now cope with—without parental assistance. Retired University of Chicago ethicist, Don S. Browing, found that "among all the conflicting transformations energized by modernization and globalization, the most ominous is the growing alienation of males from families, from the children they have fathered, and from the women who have given birth to their offspring."[38]

Another mark against the Black male in relation to Black marriage is that fewer of them are available for marriage than ever before. Why?

1. Incarceration.

2. Higher prospects for interracial marriage for Black men.

3. The vigorous shift in the purse-wallet (economics) situation we cited earlier between Black men and women in America.

R. R. Banks exposes how these contributors to the shortage of Black men further aggravate the marriage rate and success among blacks.

> First, black men incarceration constricts the market for poor and working-class black women. Second, interracial marriage depletes the pool of men for middle-class, college-educated black women. Third, the economic prospects for many men have worsened while those for women have improved. This

economic repositioning is most apparent among African Americans, but it extends throughout our society.[39]

These factors sway the interpersonal relations between Black men and women. They impact the internal conditioning of the Black male for marriage, whether he hopes to marry within or outside of his race. They also affect the hearts, minds, and beliefs of black women who desire to marry within their race. In discussing the horrible fallout incarceration has on Blacks' marriage option, Banks observes that although African Americans make up only fifteen percent of the entire U.S. population, black males bear the highest incarceration rate of any ethnic group in America. Black males are seven percent of the population in America. Yet forty-two percent of the inmates in American prisons are black males. Of two million inmates, 840,000 are black males. Can you see the hit on Black marriage? It's not hard to miss.

Michelle Alexander, civil rights lawyer, advocate, legal scholar, law professor and author states:

> Nothing has contributed more to the systemic mass incarceration of people of color [Blacks and Hispanics] in the United States than the War on Drugs … one in every fourteen black men was behind bars in 2006, compared with one in 106 white men … For young black men, the statistics are even worse. One in nine black men between the ages of twenty and thirty-five was behind bars in 2006, and far more were under some form of penal control such as probation or parole.[40]

Banks corroborates a similar claim that is devastating on Black men and women and their potential for matrimony. He says,

> At any given time, one in ten black men in their early thirties is incarcerated, and for men in their early twenties, the incarceration rate is closer to one in eight. Some researchers have estimated that more than a quarter of all black men will spend some time in prison. Black men are eight times as likely as white men to be incarcerated.[41]

The risk of prison or jail is linked a good deal to a man's socio-economic status. But the damage to Black men and women hoping or planning to marry or a Black couple already married yet dealing with spousal incarceration is clear. As for interracial coupling, not everyone endorses what is widely accepted to be the biblical view of marriage. That is, marriage between a man and woman is not only honorable but can be experienced and enjoyed between all ethnicities. Thankfully, the Lord celebrates ethnic and economic diversity in marriage as He does diversity in people and people groups.

The three factors identified above that contribute to the man and marriage shortage in the Black community cause a lot of internal angst among Black men. Arguably, even more angst is experienced among Black women who want to marry within their race. Many Black women in general are angry at Black men for their absence and the depth of relational fallout between them. Veroff and colleagues stress the importance of context when noting that African American couples "interpret their marital experiences in the context of their social worlds, their kin and their economic situations—all within a backdrop of institutional racism."[42]

It's not far-fetched, then, to assume that many Black men interpret their personal and interpersonal marital experience, or the prospect for one, through their ability: a) to get or keep a job or not; b) to earn or steal a decent salary; c) to stay out or stay put in jail; d) to deal effectively or not with racism; and e) to raise or run from their children.

The list can go on and on, depending upon how a Black male may or may not interpret and interact with his environment from the inside-out. Even with all that in mind, perhaps the only person in America who can come close to identifying with the experience of the Black man is the *Black woman.* Which leads me to ask what's the primary core longing(s) that Black women face and why?

The Primary Core Longing(s) of Black Women in Marriage

It's no secret within the African American community that heterosexual Black women are quite un-partnered when it comes to marriage. In the January 24, 2010 issue of *The Tennessean,* a local newspaper in Nashville, an article entitled "*Marriage Eludes Many Black Women*" reported that forty-six percent of Black women have not tied the knot versus twenty-three percent of White women. Not only are the numbers twice as high for these women but the pain and broken promises of matrimony are even higher. As of 2022, the issue has worsened. Take for instance, Elisha Holt, a mother of four who says "I used to break down crying when I would hear about other people getting married … I would think, why can't that be me? Or Melanie Crouch, who owns her own home, has a fulfilling career as a middle school teacher, has more pairs of heels than a small shoe store. But acknowledges just about the only thing missing from her life is a husband. And as an African American woman in Nashville, she doesn't like her odds of finding one."[43]

Elisha's and Melanie's sentiments represent Black women in every sector of American life. Some of this statistical fallout relative to Black women is attributed to the over-incarceration of black males, the greater incidence of interracial marriage, and the dramatic shift in the financial balance of power between Black men and women. How do these and other negative realities impact or damage the Black woman's psyche in or for marriage? Richardson and Wade extracted key insight from Wade's professional experience from her work with Black women in her private practice, retreats, and workshops. A segment of their book called *Our Emotional Inheritance* recognizes fourteen "inner being" beliefs which they believe arise from Black women's collective and entire experience in coming to and being in America. The first seven of those fourteen beliefs they categorize as "anti-intimacy" beliefs resident in the souls of many Black women today:

> There will never be enough of anything I need, especially love. I am not good enough to be loved. I will lose anyone who gets close to me. It is not safe for me to face my anger. No matter what I do, it will not make a difference. I have to control everyone and everything around me to protect myself from being hurt again. My body is not my own.[44]

These anti-intimacy beliefs are all lies. Worse yet, these lies tend to cover up more deviant lies. Other lies like, I do not believe these lies are real or can be part of my reality. And if they are real, surely these lies are not as destructive to me or to my marriage as some would have me to believe.

Sista! It is all a lie. Furthermore, it can be concluded that Black women's search for answers to their core-longing deficits is in part due to the current plight of Black men in America and its internal and interpersonal impact on them as women. It must also be argued that the residue from past infractions of slavery and present-day racism and sexism, executed largely but not solely by White men on Black women in America, contribute to the struggle of core-longings in Black women. It is quite easy to see why and how Black women harbor anti-intimacy beliefs on such a widespread basis. These anti-intimacy beliefs are also surnamed "limiting beliefs" by Richardson and Wade.[45] Viewing this through the lens of Wardle's structures of healing, such beliefs appear to fit into the classification of "false beliefs."

Of the leading well-known psychologists, professors, therapists, marriage counselors, caregivers, pastors, pastoral counselors, and researchers on marriage familiar to me, like Andrey Chapman, Kumea Shorter-Gooden, T.D. Jakes, John Gottman, Les and Leslie Parrot, and numerous others, they all tout that intimacy, mainly emotional intimacy, is the core priority for most any female in marriage. Likely more important for the typical Black woman, given how her historical and often present-day experience are influenced by the mitigating factors above. Confronted with this truth, does anyone, particularly husbands, need to wonder why God directs us husbands "to love our wives as Christ loved the church" (Ephesians 5:25)?

Shaunti Feldhahn penned a book for men about women from surveys of thousands of women. She discovered that the number one concern that matters most for women is "reassurance." Feldhahn found that "women have an underlying *insecurity* about whether their man (husband), for that matter fiancé or boyfriend, really loves them."[46] The harsher reality that Black women face makes this matter of reassurance or security an even more pressing concern for them.

Richardson and Wade argue that the limiting beliefs Black women harbor are often compounded by them "attracting or being attracted to men or lovers with similar beliefs and behaviors."[47] In such cases, the filling of core-longing deficits is likely dismal at best and doomed at worse. Again, relevant to this discussion of Black women and core-longings is the application of what one study revealed about Black men and Black women. You may recall that researchers determined that the sexes interpret their marital experiences, both emotional and non-emotional, in the context of their social worlds, etc., all within the backdrop of institutional racism. It seems rational, then, to assume that Black women's interpretation of their expectations in marriage would be quite different from that of Black men.

Picking up on a factor identified earlier, on average Black men are now worse off when it comes to education and economics than Black women.[48] Thus, not only might Black women have to deal with the Black male ego because he is not the breadwinner or interested in being the breadwinner in marriage, but he may have to grapple with a negative attitude or perception exuded by the Black female who is the breadwinner. For sure, one way or another, for good or bad, their self-identity and self-esteem will be impacted by the notion of the Black male having been benched as the breadwinner—if he ever was that. What about the Black female "balling" as the breadwinner? This was unheard of in previous generations of Black marriages and rarely existed in White marriages.

This, again, brings up the following question. What core longing(s) might this suggest tends to dominate Black women in general in the context of marriage? The authorities on male and female relations have much more to point out concerning this. First, keep in mind the negative affect(s) of the yo-yo or with-withdrawal approach to Black male-female personal and interpersonal relationships highlighted earlier. Much, but not all of it, is more often caused by the behavior of Black men. To exacerbate already burgeoning core-longing challenges against Black marriage, today Black women as mothers shoulder the bulk of the child-rearing and head-of-household duties within the African American community. Studies show that most Black babies are now born out of wedlock irrespective of the socioeconomics of black women and black men.[49] Of course, this fact of itself does not automatically mean fatherlessness looms ahead for the Black children involved. For most, not so. For others it is so. And what of the squandered marital opportunities? God forbid that many Black women grow weary and give up on raising their children. Then African Americans and America would be in a devastating situation.

H. P. McAdoo reveals this recent development in the black community. In 1960, only twenty-two percent of black babies were born out of wedlock.[50] Today that number hovers around seventy percent. Depending upon the study you read, it could be as high as seventy-five percent with no end in sight. A November 7, 2010 article, written in *The Tennessean*, titled *Debate Flares over Unwed Black*

Mothers, compared the Black community's seventy percent out-of-wedlock birth rates to seventeen percent among Asians, twenty-nine percent among whites, fifty-three percent among Hispanics, and sixty-six percent among Native Americans. The article cited a powerful observation from OB-GYN, Dr. Natalie Carroll, who has spent a career helping Black women in Houston. Dr. Carroll said "the girls (Black girls) don't think they have to get married. I (Dr. Carroll) tell them children deserve a mama and a daddy."[51]

I have one caveat to add. Just as many Black boys and men behave the same way when it comes to children. Although the problem is not exclusive to Blacks, Blacks do lead the way.

We also must take into consideration unacknowledged and unresolved issues and situations in which many Black women may have been born and raised. For example, single parent households without fathers or Black men. The current and future impact such strong anomaly has on Black children as they become adults, who will marry or want to, is worrisome. One set of caregivers' reason that "women who were abandoned in childhood, by one or both parents, are often attracted to mates who end up deserting them physically and emotionally."[52] These negative influences flow from one generation to another, arousing the emergence of core-longing deficits in Black women as they attempt to interact with men who look and act like their own fathers.

One lawyer recorded that "black women are only half as likely as white women to be married, and more than three times as likely as white women never to marry."[53] While many, including myself, do not condone premarital sex, cohabitation or "shacking-up" as it is commonly referred to. The lawyer also noted that Black women are even three times as likely as White women to not have an intimate partner for all the reasons cited above by him and the other thinkers.[54]

The evidence trail strongly indicates that the typical Black married woman and Black single woman who desires marriage feels shortchanged when it comes to the essential core longing of *security*. Her core longing for security is rooted in love as much as the Black man's core longing to belong is. Can you imagine droves of Black women asking on their way to the altar or past it: Can I trust this Black man to secure my heart in his connection with the Lord? Can I trust him to secure our parenting together or even to have and hold kids with me? Can I trust him and me to be secure in what I bring to the table financially, even if my purse bests his wallet? Can I be secure that he will stay home and not be behind jail bars? Can I trust him to not leave me "un-partnered" in holy matrimony?

In addition to all this, many Black women and their husbands have an even greater question: Why is there so much inner turmoil in and between us? This leads me to question what psychodynamics and other factors impair Black men and women, or those engaged to be married from inquiring about and addressing their core-longings and the defeat that may plague them?

Other Factors That Impair Core Longings of Black Married Couples

It's one thing to have a core-longing problem. It's quite another to be unaware that you have a problem or why you have it. Interestingly, people often "feel" there is a problem within them before they "know" what it is or "know why" one exists. Many Black spouses as individuals do not often realize the value in making sense of their life.[55] For core longings to be experienced, there must entail what might be termed as a "core learning (inquiry)" journey to unpack the meaning of behaviors of, and on, the individual relative to core longings.

Black Married Couples Confronting the Past as Present

Due to the stigma or pain associated with a past and a present impacted by slavery, racism, classism, and other "isms" for Black men and women, as well sexism for Black women, Blacks are often skeptical or cynical of "looking back." A common refrain in the Black community is "leave the past in the past" or "leave the past behind." The problem is the past and its pain are notorious for not leaving itself or anyone behind. They both tend to stay with people who have not confronted them properly.

As we saw, Black men and women have the frequent habit of 1) keeping family secrets, 2) keeping up appearances [like the couple in our earlier illustration], and 3) waiting until problems reach the crisis point before contending with how the past and present impact the now.[56] All these bad habits are reasons why core-longing deficits stay arrested in Blacks. One of the first things Black men and women need to do as they begin this core-learning journey is revisit in their hearts, minds, and memory those issues generated in their family-of-origin. Richardson and Wade assert that "love relationships often mirror those of our parents because behaviors are passed on inter-generationally, from grandparent to parent to child. Everyone, regardless of race [or gender], acts out an emotional script that was written generations before by our ancestors."[57] Even if they must revisit multiple generations due to family secrets, etc., Black men and women must learn to live with the fact that the past has redemptive value if revisited right.

Other researchers identify a similar pattern in the parent-child relationship. Many adults as parents object to revisiting their childhood because they feel it is too time-consuming. Yet they may wonder why their parenting style with their own children is similar to or lacking what they were exposed to as kids. Parents can ill-afford not to take the time to revisit their family-of-origin experiences and memories that may inform their parenting.[58]

McNeal also contends that it's hard to develop the self if one lacks self-awareness or understanding.[59] Self-awareness is vital for the Black couple and each Black spouse to address given that Blacks own a unique history and set of modern distractions influencing their internal and interpersonal make up. Another restraint on core longings for engaged or married Black men and women is unresolved "bad" beliefs carried into their marriages.

Black Married Couples Confronting Limiting Beliefs

"Limiting beliefs," "false beliefs," or what I call "our mentals" refers to our beliefs, feelings, and behaviors that shape our mental/emotional/spiritual self. Unless rectified, they exert damaging control on the interrelatedness between Black married couples and engaged folk. Boyd-Franklin, Richardson and Wade, Bryant and others all concede that such bad beliefs may stem from how Black men and women were and are socialized amid various societal factors. For instance, Boyd-Franklin cites the notion that

Black boys are often taught they cannot show "weakness" and Black girls are told they must be "self-reliant."[60] Thus, the BET or modern mantra, "Black girls rock!" In fact, Black fathers nowadays raise their daughters to be self-reliant. My mind reminisces on a friend of mine, who emphatically stated, "I raised my Black adult daughter to live independently of a Black man." I think he meant any man. But we get the point.

On the other end, Black boys are often raised under the pretentious notion that they are to be resilient regardless of the costs, oddity, or odious nature of their circumstances. What then do Black men or women do when they both need to cry? Such beliefs undermine intimacy or closeness by stoking emotional isolation in Black couples via Black individualism. I am of the persuasion that way too many Blacks in marriage or engaged—especially young couples—sabotage the chance to thrive in marriage out of a distorted sense of "self-reliance" and a need to "arrive." They opt to go or be somewhere (professionally or otherwise) that their relational skill, will, or relationship cannot help or support them. For example, trying to ascend, too quickly, to the top rung professionally as a new adult in a new marriage, especially one with young children, is a near enigma. Relationally, this is a death wish.

Black Married Couples and Intimacy

Wrong beliefs distort the emotional attunement and attachment process of man to woman in marriage and parent to child in family. Two experts on attachment theory define emotional attunement and attachment from the standpoint of the parent-child relationship as:

> The alignment of one's internal state with the primary emotions of another that links them into a state of emotional resonance that enables the other person to 'feel felt.' By attachment it is meant the sense of well-being that emerges from predictable and repeated experiences of care whereby people feel secure with another.[61]

We can and must parallel this to adult relationships because Halley urges that as caregivers, attunement and attachment are critically "important to understand when considering how to assess and care for the wounded child who is living within a wounded adult."[62] For the Black individual or couple who suffers wounded like a child, it is important for them to embrace their feelings, to experience being "felt," and to know that someone understands and can help—if they seek it. Consequently, characterizing such wounded people as "grown" but not "grown-up," at least not emotionally, would be rather insightful. This is often due to childhood trauma.

It is my assumption that for Black couples, the presence of childhood trauma (either latent or being lived out) in the man or woman or both tends to be higher compared to other groups, based on the circumstances that we have already outlined. Couples need to recognize their failure to attune and attach, then discover why. Attunement and attachment are crucial for married adults as well as others. Two essential realities can "access and activate the negative consequences of a wounded child within a wounded adult: 1) Experience of adult trauma, and 2) *Intimate relationships.*"[63] Poor attachment and attunement can exploit unhealed wounds in spouses and engaged folk, causing implosion or explosion in married couples' relations. This underscore why it is vital that couples are helped by Spirit-led and skilled caregivers. They can assist the couple to make sense, or get an understanding of their lives, as written in the Bible in Proverbs 4:7.

Black Married Couples Making Sense of Their Lives

In the powerful book *Parenting from the Inside Out,* the authors link the presence or worsening of core-longing deficit(s) to a person's lack of self-understanding. They assert that without self-understanding, no individual or couple, including Black couples, can begin to make sense of their lives.[64] What people believe or understand about themselves can be life changing. And that is because beliefs morph into behaviors. Behaviors often morph into destructive habits. Destructive habits morph into addictive patterns of behaving (doing), thinking, feeling and being.[65] This leads to a de-emphasis and disconnect of core longings.

One psychiatrist and child development expert claims that self-understanding can propel a person a long way into asking, finding, and getting answers to not only tough, but as one Christian minister advocates, the right questions being asked of self by self and others. Questions like 1) why do I work so hard to seek others' approval? Or, 2) am I overly compliant because I am afraid to hurt others' feelings?[66]

Without question, self-understanding helps spouses to discover, discern, and decide whether to adopt healthy versus unhealthy healing practices. This is particularly of value for Black couples who researchers say are typically unaccustomed or inexperienced in seeking outside help, as compared to White couples. So, what outside sources have blacks historically relied on to help overcome such internal deficiency and accompanying marital dissatisfaction? More importantly, how in the world do Blacks reclaim our successful history of marriage in America that has become so sullied over the past fifty or so years? In the next segment, we will place a spotlight on some of the main healing opportunities and tools that exist to help married and engaged blacks address their core longing needs.

Chapter 3

Black Men and Women Strive to Reclaim the Marriage Option

Bishop T.D. Jakes, a well-known preacher and prolific writer, asks two penetrating questions from a story in his book, *Loose That Man and Let Him Go.*

> What prompts a forty-year-old man to suddenly discover one night as he lies in bed that he needs to be held? All of his life he's been the holder. All of a sudden this macho man turns to his wife and says, just hold me. When the pain breaks through, we are wrestled to the ground and made to face an unsettling fact: A hurting little boy still lives within. We cannot divorce ourselves from our inner need. So how do we spell relief?[67]

From my vantage point, there exist four avenues that can lead to restoration when the marriage option has been crippled by core-longing deficits. *Counseling. Clergy. The Church. Concentrated group support.*

Black Married Couples and Traditional Counseling/Psychotherapy

Black couples have historically relied mostly on themselves to police their relationships. Their resistance to traditional forms of counseling or psychotherapy treatment is partly "due to an emphasis on keeping up appearances. This is further complicated by the abundance of family secrets in many black families. They tend to work extremely hard to hide their problems from others."[68] If a Black couple does opt to enter a counseling setting (and it is a big if), that's no guarantee they overcame their resistance. It simply might manifest in a different manner. For instance, they might sporadically show up for counseling sessions. Or they might not be forthright or transparent with their counselor or each other in sessions.

Sometimes the resistance to therapy in Black couples is one-sided. From my experience, it's typically on the part of the male. It's not at all unusual during an initial consult that a counselor must ask, "Does your spouse agree to attend and participate in counseling"? And often the counselor will have to assuage the person's suspicions about the process before going forward, or once counseling starts. This resistant behavior is generally not true of wives. At least, this has not been my experience working with Black couples and couples in general. Nevertheless, in my opinion, the help that counseling can provide for married Black couples is worth taking the risk of working through their resistance in order to enjoy the reward of a sound marriage.

Black Married Couples and Clergy

I have seen for myself that a pastor, over and above traditional counselors, has a better chance of seeing and helping Blacks in their marriages. This is due to the continuous, informal, non-clinical, pastor-parishioner relationship they share.[69] As a pastor of a Black urban church, over a period of eighteen or so years now, I have witnessed Black couples' unfamiliarity with and resistance to traditional forms of therapy. Yet these same couples are mostly receptive to counseling from a pastor. Even so, the struggle is real. Clergy must be willing to offer a counseling approach that is informal, intermittent, and not as structured as traditional counseling. It might need to happen in various phases and ways. A little bit here. A lot of bit there. Otherwise, it could be viewed as a threat in the hearts and minds of the Black couple striving to resurrect or begin their marital life.

> According to surveys, over sixty percent of Americans prefer to see clergy about personal problems such as marital trouble and family difficulties. The demand for individual and marital counseling from pastors is likely to increase.[70]

Many Blacks who turn to their clergy for help do so because they perceive traditional forms of therapy as "White." One Sista named Rosemary, who was in a very broken black marriage said when encouraged to seek counseling that "therapy was for crazy white girls."[71] However, there is good news. The antagonism toward traditional counseling and therapy in the eyes of Black individuals and couples is steadily changing. One primary reason is because mental healthcare toward Blacks in and outside of marriage has morphed considerably within the last half-century. According to Harold Koenig, one pivotal way today's church has increased its concern and care for couples is in the sheer number of counseling hours clergy spend helping others within the church. Ten to twenty percent of their forty-to-sixty-hour work week is spent counseling those with emotional or marital problems.

> Survey of 635 African American congregations in the northeastern United States found that eighteen percent of church-based programs involved some form of counseling for members.[72]

As a pastor and minister for twenty-five plus years I can attest to this fact. Few within my own congregation realize that counseling absorbs much of my pastoral work and at times keeps me quite busy. McMurry and Worthington predicted this growth nearly thirty years ago. The demand for individual and marital counseling from pastors is likely to increase. One reason for the likely increase is economic. Insurance companies may not reimburse psychotherapists for marital counseling because marital distress is not considered a health problem. The cost of therapy from professionals can range from $60 to $125 per hour. For most people, that's prohibitively high. Most pastors do not charge for counseling.[73] Nowadays, more insurance companies cover the cost of marriage counseling. These changes have resulted in more direct redress of the core longings of married and engaged Blacks.

Black Married Couples and the Church

Africans who were captured and brought to America as slaves were:

> dispossessed of their complex culture and familiar social customs. The process of dehumanizing began immediately and was continued consistently until the slaves' arrival in the New World and subsequent purchase by a white owner . . . The close-knit family and tribal associations they had once enjoyed were destroyed. Familiar customs relating to their work and religion became a vague memory, as did former systems of kinship and organized social life.[74]

The core longings of these enslaved Africans or Blacks were strategically and maliciously battered by slave traders and slave owners. Nevertheless, it was against the backdrop of the crucible of slavery that the early Black church originated. Raboteau highlights that "by the Eve of the Civil War, Christianity or a Christ-centered religious fervor had pervaded the slave community."[75] Remarkably what started out as a forced religion and practice among slaves by slaveowners, became an authentic and dominant faith belief and practice among the slave and ex-slave community: *Christianity*. But how specifically did the Black church in this period help alleviate the plight of enslaved blacks, whether in pseudo (non-legal) marriage or not?

For the slaves who worked and suffered in an alien

world, religion offered a means of catharsis for their 'pent-up emotions and frustrations'. Moreover, it turned their minds from the sufferings and privations of this world to a world after death where the weary would find rest and the victims of injustices would be compensated.[76]

An organized religious life became the chief means by which a structured or organized social life came into existence among the Negro masses.

In providing a structured social life in which the Negro could give expression to his *'deepest feeling'* and at the same time achieve status and *'find a meaningful existence'*, the Negro church provided a refuge in a hostile white world. What mattered was the way he [or she] was treated in the church which gave him [or her] an opportunity for self-expression and status. He or she could always find an escape from such, often *painful*, experiences within the shelter of his or her church.[77]

Scholars explain that while usually denied the chance to train scientifically or medically to be a mental-health provider, the one unique personality/person/professional who largely fulfilled the caregiving role to Blacks was *the Black minister*. Contrary to the notorious myths about the Black male, the Black minister was quite effective and accepted not only because of his "calling from God," but also because he was typically a homegrown product of the experience of the Black community he served. Due to this natural or cultural affinity and whatever gifts he had as a preacher-pastor-leader-sage-caregiver-untrained but God-gifted counselor; the Black minister, often barely literate and certainly not trained in the latest psychological theory or techniques, was nevertheless: *impactful and irreplaceable*.[78] And he or she still is! Blank, Mahmood, Fox, and Guterbock referred to these ministerial caregivers as "natural helpers," along with family and friends, situated within the Black community.

Another historian acknowledged that the Black preacher "was the most visible, most influential, and often most powerful spiritual guide, moral leader, teacher, and disciplinarian in the community that he mirrored.[79] Only God knows the depth to which the Black church in this period undertook to minister to its hurting people. Both the American public and African Americans owe a vast debt of gratitude for the effort and efficacy of the Black church.

The Black church and Black folk in general owe a greater debt of gratitude to Jesus for enabling the Black church in this way. The Black church, with the Lord's help, did nothing short of the miraculous, in my view, to curtail the devastating effect of core-longing defeat and brokenness in the hearts, minds, and souls of Black men and women. Of course, all this action helped supply a humanitarian uplift which served to catapult Blacks' marital purposes and overall aims in the right direction.

The Black church has, often with little to no help from mainstream America, sought to soothe the emotional cries and crisis of its community and congregants. However, one thinker reports that today the church offers people access to an evolving web of mental health service through what he calls "FBO's" or faith-based organizations. These FBO's are classified into five categories:

1) local religious congregations, 2) networking and advocacy groups that support and educate congregations to help those with severe mental illness, 3) national organizations tied financially/administratively to a religious group that provide mission-driven social services, 4) groups that deliver faith-based mental health services, but are not connected to a local or national religious group, and 5) religious counselors who focus on religious therapies like Christian counseling, etc.[80]

If you are honest, and if you or someone you know has a marital need or other mental health issue, which of the FBO's or faith-based organizations do you need to tap into as a married individual or couple? And does your church have or desire any sort of FBO presence?

Black Marriage and Concentrated Small Group Support

The small group approach to help Black men and women tackle matrimonial issues is a novel approach. Consequently, they might be less willing to try it, given the fact that (1) it's relatively new, (2) Blacks tend to prefer privacy, but secrecy is not conducive to small group participation, and (3) it's a less available form of help for Blacks in marriage. However, I believe concentrated small group therapy offers Blacks who are married or engaged a credible source of support… if used properly. Biblically speaking, God began His involvement in human affairs through small group activity. He did so through a husband and wife named Adam and Eve. At the dawn of the church period, Jesus began His work in the early church with a small group of twelve original disciples. Each of these small group initiatives, stoked by God, continue to yield undeniable influence and impact on the world stage.

The acceptable size of a small group is six to ten members.[81] The purpose of an Afrocentric encounter group would be for engaged or married individuals who are alienated or broken to encounter God in Christ individually and as a couple, thereby transforming their marital pain and problems into gain. In church lingo, we might say the goal is for a "deliverance or breakthrough" that only Christ can bring with an outcome that favorably affects their marital future.

Also, this small group effort is expected to address healing elements. From Yalom's purview, there exists ten healing elements paramount to effective group therapy. They are:

> The impartation of information, instillation of hope, universality [*participants need to know they are not alone nor are their problems unique*], altruism, the corrective recapitulation of the primary family group, development of socializing techniques, imitative behavior, interpersonal learning, group cohesiveness, and catharsis.[82]

For church going, born again Christians, seeking to heal or succeed in marriage, there is an eleventh healing element. It's really our first and foremost healing element: *Jesus!* His name has unparalleled power, presence, and purpose. One wise presbyterian pastor and biblical small group expert identifies the first group known to God and humanity. This small, yet supernatural and sacred group is the Father, Son, and Holy Spirit, which is known as the Trinity or Godhead.

The late Howard Clinebell believes that "group-caring and counseling methods constitute the single most useful resource for broadening and deepening a church's ministry of healing and growth. These caring and counseling methods can find their expression in five types of church groups: a) task, service and action groups; b) study groups; c) supportive-inspirational groups [including corporate worship]; d) growth groups; and e) crisis counseling and therapy groups."[83]

Donna Thomas, an adjunct professor at Ashland Theological Seminary and a small group specialist in formational counseling, says Christ-oriented small groups, particularly healing care groups, offer wounded people three awesome forms of support: "1) A group is God's design for transformation, 2) It's a biblical and theological view on community and most urgently, 3) A group is where Jesus dwells [and meets people]."[84] Jesus Himself said in Matthew 18:20, "for where two or three are gathered together in my name, I am there among them." Who in the church and in crisis-mode does not want to meet Jesus for help? Thomas summarizes her argument by affirming that basically,

> Both science and psychotherapeutic research
> report what the Bible [the Trinity and church]
> has attested to since the beginning of time:
> gathering together for mutual support in the
> presence of a safe and empathic caregiver is
> necessary for emotional healing and growth.[85]

No wonder we are told in the scripture "in the abundance of counsel there is victory and safety." (Proverbs 11:14). No wonder God gave Adam, Eve. He made them a couple. A small unit. A small team. A small group. A marriage. Not simply mates on a date. No wonder Moses sent twelve spies, a small group, to scout out the enemy's position. No wonder Jesus had twelve original disciples, a small group of ministers He personally, pastorally trained and sent out two by two or in groups of three at times... a small group. No wonder the Bible says two are better than one, and that a three-fold cord cannot be easily broken. Clearly, there is power, promise, protection, prevention, and prime strength, endorsed by the Lord, inherent in small group work or ministry.

I agree with Julie Gorman, author of two small group studies, when she asserts that "the purpose of a small group is not meetings but maturity, not making connections as much as knowing God. True spiritual community leads to growth ... and she believes that the Spirit of God is the agent of formation within group."[86] Black church goers receive predominant and proficient group support in the areas that Clinebell calls task-service or action groups (men/women's ministry), study groups (Bible) and supportive-inspirational groups (choir), including corporate worship.

But in Clinebell's latter two groups—growth, crisis counseling and therapy groups—into which marital small group falls, the support is not proficient. When it comes to Encounter Groups, others might argue the support is usually not prevalent nor proficient for Blacks toward marriage. My hope is that the effort behind this book will help reverse this stubborn trend. If we are to protect and recover Blacks' collective marriage option, there simply needs to be widespread prevention/restorative practices expressed in small group ministry targeting Blacks' marriage interest. I'd much rather we offer wide scale marriage care than divorce care small groups in the church. And I certainly hope that most individuals would prefer this, too.

There is a disturbing trend involving Blacks and their group participation. Research shows that when it comes to human service groups or personal growth groups, participation by Black men and women has in recent decades often been more *"involuntary and court mandated"* than voluntary and church-sanctioned or even community-sponsored.[87]

Looking at this from my ministry experience, far more is needed if there is to be a serious push toward small group ministry targeting married Black folk.

The average black church does not have a small group ministry or any substantive small group cohort for Blacks readying for or reeling in marriage and needing restoration.

Professional comrades of Smith College Student Counseling Service contend that any surge in small-group activity inside or outside the church should be powered by four key healing factors. They say these four therapeutic touches are necessary for ethnic minorities in group work. These healing factors include: "validation, empowerment, self-empathy and mutuality."[88] That is still a goal to be reached, as Clinebell says, and I agree, "we have not even scratched the surface" here yet.

Chapter 4

Black Men and Women Situated to Relay Small Group Aid to the Marriage Option

We have highlighted that from the pre-war times extending late into the twentieth century, the American community and church had neither the will nor the psychological skill to address the problems of Blacks. Today it has both the skill and will to help. One relatively unknown but exciting branch of this psychological skill is called formational counseling or inner healing prayer.

Developed by caregiver, former pastor, and seminary professor, Rev. Dr. Terry Wardle, formational counseling has a prayer component and is grounded in reliance on the Holy Spirit. This ministry approach is useful to Blacks' marriage hopes because it offers: 1) an integrated view on caregiving, 2) a reversal from "pastor-led" to Spirit-led care facilitated by pastors and laymen, 3) inner healing prayer, and 4) a fresh ministry model for addressing wounds by means of a concentrated small group.

I believe a formational counseling centered small group is an ideal way to introduce small group ministry to Blacks in or outside the church who are in, or headed into marriage. Formational counseling "does not see Christianity (theology) and counseling (psychology) as functioning independently in different spheres."[89] Rather, both God-given "ologies" are brought to bear on the playing field of the human heart and its hurt. Black men and women in emotional pain often over-rely on their pastors for help. But not all pastors wish to, or know how to, integrate theology and psychology. This is vital, however, since a theological view, a psychological view, and even pastoral intervention alone can only go so far in its ability to "confront and cure" both the cause and contributing forces to wounds in wounded people.[90] This is why Wardell champions formational counseling by saying,

> It is essential that we stop marginalizing the Holy Spirit in our lives and ministries, opening up to the only power that can truly change lives."[91] Proper ranking and use of these two healing agents (pastor and Paraclete) with all involved in a healing context is vital. It should be the Spirit first, the caregiver (any) second, always. This is especially vital considering formational counseling places a huge premium on not just prayer but "inner healing prayer." And the success of inner healing prayer places an ultimate premium on the work of the Spirit.[92]

Inner healing prayer is to Christian empowerment and crisis what a strong army is to a looming war—*might*. The goal of inner healing prayer is to make Jesus (or the Spirit of Christ) "the prime mediator between God and the individual human being or couple who is hurting."[93] I wholeheartedly agree. Many hard-working pastors can use a rest from church members' over-dependence upon both pastoral and or self-representation when emotional healing is on the line.

One godly, very experienced caregiver, and care-receiver, sums up this essential need when writing, "emotional healing cannot happen apart from prayer. Not just a quick opening prayer before a session, but aggressive, multi-faceted, Spirit-filled prayer … prayer is the most essential ingredient on the pathway to inner healing."[94] The Formational Counseling Healing Care small group ministry is a relational support tool that provides "true community. . . experiencing God . . . experiencing people . . . The community arena that is small group community, provides the opportunity for spiritual transformation like none other. Participation in community also fulfills our deepest longings to belong."[95] And, as we have detailed, belonging is crucial to Black male and female well-being. I believe many Black couples would consent to participating in a group such as this for the following reasons.

1. They would have the opportunity to experience that people and marriages can grow and heal in relationship to God and others in a safe group environment.[96]

2. They would likely be receptive after seeing that by design "attention is drawn away from the practitioner (caregiver) in favor of pointing to the provision of Christ."[97]

3. They would benefit because "much of the counseling and even more of the caring (sharing), which is typically done individually, can be

done more effectively in small groups due to its communal posture."[98]

The Healing Care Group curriculum would consist of a "teaching component—based on the Word, an experiential component, and a spiritual focus all under the care of a trained facilitator working with no more than 8 to 10 participants or 4-5 black couples,"[99] done over a period of 12 weeks.

The T.D. Jakes' illustration from earlier pointed out that "we cannot divorce ourselves from our inner need." Yet people frequently use marriage as means to try to do just that. The formational counseling ministry offers Black couples a three-dimensional approach to inner healing brought about by the integration of spiritual direction, Christ-centered counseling, and formational or inner healing prayer. Sole custody of inner healing is given over to the leadership and lordship of the Spirit.[100]

Spirit-Directed Healing

Christian psychologists Cloud and Townsend confidently say that "people need two sets of relationships to grow: the divine and the human."[101] Note that they identify the divine, first, and the human, second. This is by design. Not theirs—but God's! The place and prominence of the Spirit must not be disordered or disturbed in the Spirit-directed and human-assisted agency of formational counseling. For that matter, any counseling ideally.

By utilizing a Spirit-led, empathic caregiver, to help the care-receivers (couple) gain an individual and interpersonal awareness of the presence of the Lord in their personal and relational plight, the couple hopefully allows the Spirit liberty to do with and for them what only the Spirit can. Wardle says of the Spirit and caregiver's roles that "the Holy Spirit's presence is so much more than functional. He is there to be in relationship with the caregivers."[102] The Spirit is there equally for the care-receivers. The Spirit can patrol and penetrate the hurt in those spouses or spouses-to-be who are hounded by hurt or in need of growth for marriage.

This is a different and more dynamic and biblical approach than what many Black couples are accustomed to or have encountered. As we have said, repeatedly, too many have come to rely on themselves or the strength and skill of clergy who may not be totally reverential and reliant on the person of the Holy Spirit to guide them in helping the broken persons and spouses in their care. The Spirit should be the primary helper to the caregiver. And to the care-receiver. Cloud and Townsend put it this way: "If you are helping people grow, make sure you look for how connected they are to the indwelling Christ. No matter what the issue or struggle, relatedness to the Spirit must come first. It is as important as checking the gas gauge before you leave on a car trip."[103]

Being "woke" as young folk might say, not politically but spiritually, and aware of the presence of the Lord is certainly different than being haunted by the crippling presence of "the past as a dominating presence." Many Black couples need to ask in their search for inner and inter-relational serenity, "Are we aware of His presence?"[104] Spirit-directed facilitators can help Black couples contend with their struggles. First, they can help the couples, particularly the Christian ones, grasp that the Lord is not utterly "angry" with them and/or their past, and that they need to fall in love with the heavenly Father that Jesus knows and loves[105] because He truly loves them. This would radically alter them.

Second, they can help couples with dulled senses understand that "Christianity is a sensuous faith" designed to help us experience the majesty of the Lord even amid our pain.[106] These ebony individuals coupled together in matrimony need to know that their Christ-centered faith is as good for dealing with their feelings, as with their thoughts, their soul, and the behaviors connected to them.

Third, as we have heavily concentrated on, they can help many hurting Black couples deepen their view and experience of the third person of the Trinity, the Holy Spirit. God's Holy Spirit offers a joyful, deep-abiding intimacy intertwined with a deep desire to heal their trauma. Intimacy with God through His Spirit builds intimacy with each other. Sadly, too many couples miss that fact.

The faith insights of Spirit-led facilitators will empower Black couples to do three actions essential to filling their core longings and enjoying deep intimacy. Their insights will prompt Blacks to practice (engage) the presence of the Lord through surrender, silence, and even suffering—redemptive suffering. This will help them maintain both their divine and human connections, permitting growth. This is also where Christ-centered counseling helps Black folk deal with painful memories and address false or limiting beliefs (or mentals as I call them) under the direction of the Holy Spirit.

Christian Counseling and Black Married Couples

The word therapy means "to come along side." Another important element of any Christian counseling is empathy. The ability to think, feel, understand, communicate, and connect to and through the experiences of others make up the essential ingredients of empathy. Any caregiver or counselor, whether lay or licensed, and certainly any formational counseling caregiver, can offer empathy if the desire and direction is Spirit-led and Word-based.[107] Empathy is especially important to adults harboring a frightened inner child within.[108] Yet caregivers and care-receivers must understand that empathy in counseling is most fruitful when the positioning of the caregiver toward the care-receiver is correct.

In secular mental health terminology, healthy positioning means fostering a therapeutic alliance between the counselor and client that helps therapy get along. However, in our case, the caregiver and care-receiver position themselves toward the Holy Spirit for His intent to heal. This healthy positioning gives way to healing or deliverance. The Black care-receivers' focus is taken off themselves as care-receivers and placed onto someone both parties trust to help the healing happen: *Jesus*. As each party uses the power of empathy or compassion, coupled with the caregiver's competence, positive change can take place.

Christ-centered, Christian-based counseling is also vital, given that Black couples are confronted with their own unique "neurotic vs. normal" needs in marriage. Howard Clinebell, a former professor of pastoral studies, observed that "because of severe early life need deprivation, many people bring neurotic needs, as contrasted with normal needs, to their marriages."[109] By neurotic it is not meant needs that are psychotic, just abnormal. Such abnormality does not give advantages to Black marital relations, only pitfalls and stumbling blocks. Consequently, they need counseling to help them find and form suitable ways to cope with their "intense personal needs and toxic feelings rising from others or self-rejection (feelings of inadequacy)."[110] In short, Black couples must come to terms with their true selves versus false selves, all the while trying to stay tuned to the sacredness of marriage, their marriage partner, others to some degree, and most of all, God in Christ.[111] The Spirit-led caregiver plays a big, but again, not the biggest role in enabling this interpersonal process.

For people of color, like African Americans who have historically been ostracized by enmity forces outside of its race, the idea of an empathic witness or caregiver is freeing all by itself. It certainly is freeing to me. Intentionally seeking to be empathic with people who struggle with issues of belonging, security, and rejection, is at the core of Christ-centered Christian counseling. A caregiver must remember that "no matter what the issue or struggle, relatedness must come first."[112]

Finally, an empathic caregiver (counselor) is pivotal to helping broken individuals in the art of "feeling felt," or attunement and hopefully attachment rooted in well-being. Spirit-led counseling is about helping broken people, Black individuals, and Black couples grow-up again, or to even re-parent themselves (albeit differently) under the direction of the Spirit. This includes both those who have been discounted from childhood and those who have done much to discount themselves in adulthood.[113] Anything less, and couples feel left to relationally parent one another, resulting in anomaly.

That said, few things can enable growth or healing like prayer. In Genesis 4:26, it is written that "at that time people began to call on the name of the Lord." In other words, broken people began to pray. The result: things began to change.

Formational Prayer Changes Things

There is an old saying within the Black church that "prayer changes things." Truthfully, however, that depends upon the kind of prayer, the aim, the method, and the confidence (faith) of the one praying and the one in need of prayer. Myles Munroe in his book *Understanding the Purpose and Power of Prayer* contends that people misunderstand, malign, and misappropriate prayer.[114] Blacks, particularly those married, believe in the power of prayer even though they may not appropriate it to the fullest or know the true power of the One behind it. One study found that:

> Blacks are more likely to pray during stressful circumstances than whites and that about 90% of blacks versus 60% of whites state that prayer is very important when coping with life problems. Both African American and Caribbean blacks, women and 'married' respondents were more likely to look to God for guidance than were men and women and persons who cohabit with their partners, respectively.[115]

These statistics suggest how formational counseling can offer its greatest assistance to Black engaged or married couples through its strong prayer emphasis anchored in the Spirit. Prayer in general is less threatening than counseling in the eyes of many Blacks. One reason is because prayer is often done as an individual act. However, I believe formational prayer offers a more valuable experience in prayer than some other approaches. When Black individuals and couples are dealing with leftover and unresolved issues, especially those centered around childhood issues, they need a kind of prayer ministry that can help them grow toward wholeness and that will hold them accountable to do their part to experience healing.

In the book *Strong Winds and Crashing Waves*, the author details the aim of formational prayer.

> Inner healing prayer is a work of the Holy Spirit moving through caregivers [i.e., counselor, therapist, pastor, psychologist, and laypersons, etc.] to the broken and battered. The Holy Spirit uses them to identify root wounds and to set people free from dysfunctional behaviors. He also exposes lies that bring emotional turmoil and releases the broken from demonic bondage. The Holy Spirit inspires caregivers to use scripture, confession, visualization, repentance, and healing prayer to minister grace and hope where darkness once reigned. All of this inner healing is possible because Jesus Christ has won the victory over all forms of brokenness and is available to all who turn to Him. Caregivers are not separated from the process. They are always integrated participants in the healing encounter with Christ.[116]

I believe this is the kind of prayer that changes not just things but people, broken people. All within the context of a small group setting.

Summary

I hope you have been able to see the help that Christian counseling, clergy, the church, and concentrated small groups provide concerning the cause of Christ toward the brokenhearted in marriage. In order for married African American couples or those heading into marriage to conquer and heal from the impact of core-longing deficits, caregivers and care-receivers must be determined to do several things.

First, whether in or outside of the church, they must gain a culturally sensitive and accurate understanding of (1) the African American history of struggle, abandonment, and rejection in America; (2) how that played itself out in their marriage world; (3) how that has caused or contributed to a corporate sense of core-longing deficit in Black men and women; and (4) consequently, the negative impact on Black male/female marital relations.

Caregiver and care-receivers must recognize that Black men and women are also victimized by issues of belonging for men and security for women, which are imposed on them from outside forces. Second, Black husbands and wives must ask and answer the question: what lessons of love and intimacy were passed down from my foremothers or forefathers to me, and how do I best deal with it?[117] As Richardson and Wade reveal, "the past as a presence" has left a powerful, penetrating, and seemingly inescapable "discounting" mark on the Black male and female psyche. And this psyche must daily contend with "love relationships that are often mirrored in those of Blacks' fore-parents."

Third, caregivers and care-receivers must be intellectually, emotionally, and spiritually aware of how and where Black couples go to get help for their internal and interpersonal troubles. This is crucial because marital troubleshooting for Black couples tends to take place at home or with clergy at church—or not at all. The formational counseling small-group experience called Healing Care Group is a valuable tool for addressing core longing issues in Black matrimony. If you and your spouse/fiancée or couples you know are interested in joining a Christ-centered small group experience for marriage, you can contact me at roosewalker1@aol.com.

I want to end these first four chapters by sharing a story told by Black married parents of their young son. It captures the importance of core-longing care and regulation.

> It was a weekday morning with our children hurriedly preparing for school. My husband, Mark and I were already preoccupied with details of the hectic day ahead. Just as we were about to rush out the front door, our eight-year-old son, Mark Jr., yelled, "Prayer!" and we thrust backpacks and bags out of the way. Arms circling one another, we bowed our heads. This was not the first time we'd interrupted the morning dash to pray, but it was the first time I could remember Mark Jr. being anxious to participate in a prayer. Just as we were finishing, little Mark stared meaningfully at me and then at his dad and said, "Thanks so much, God, for a mom and dad who love each other." My husband squeezed my hand. That scene occurred more than three years ago and was just a pause in

a busy day, but I will always remember it as the official turning point in my life; after a lifetime of longing for lasting love, I knew we had created it. Mark and I have now been married for fifteen years, but in our early years together, we lost too much time in angry, tense moments.[118]

This Black couple, their marriage, their treatment of their marriage option, and their son, Mark Jr., will likely continue to be healthy and happy because their core longings have been filled. No engaged or married man or woman has to continue living with core-longing deficits because such loss can be avoided or alleviated by the Word of God or the Bible. Though many Blacks relish this sacred book, they often do not rely on it, as they could and should, to favor their marriage option. Do the Bible and theology identify with or respond to the marital plight of Blacks to help them either gain, retain, or purposely work to reclaim their God-given, time-honored marital option? For that matter, might the Bible even back the healing aims/tenets of formational counseling or inner healing prayer relative to Blacks? The answer to both questions, I believe, is a resounding yes. The following chapter explain why.

Chapter 5

Black Men and Women Sensible to Rely on Bible Support of the Marriage Option

We have explored in detail that black couples grapple daily with their own variation and veracity of core-longing deficits. Recall that by core longings we mean that at the inmost being of every individual there exists a God-given longing to experience an abiding sense of belonging, love, purpose, security, significance, and understanding. These core longings are met by individuals, particularly through the primary relationships in our lives. In some sense they are even attended to by our own valuing of self. When our core longings are being fulfilled by others or self, core-longing care and fulfillment is occurring.

The words "core longings" or "core-longing maintenance and regulation" are not found specifically in the Bible. However, both Old and New Testament scriptures strongly reflect the concept. They include:

1. The Song of Songs, which provides a Black marital model of belonging, love, and security.

2. Proverbs 31, which applauds a Black marital model of purpose, significance, and understanding.

3. Matthew 19, which contains Jesus' summons to a softening of hearts (affections) in, and between spouses.

God is concerned about marriage and the individual and marital strain and pain that can stem from a lack of core-longing care in marriage. It is helpful for blacks to see this portrayed through characters in the Bible, in hopes that it will help them play it out in their own marriage space.

The Black Marital Model of Belonging, Love, and Security

In the Song of Songs, a couple avows their abiding emotional love, not just sexual love, to each other. They are apparently a couple of color. J. Daniel Hays in his work *From Every People and Nation: A Biblical Theology of Race* says "the Old Testament was completely multi-ethnic, and that it is probably safe to conclude that the Israelites of the Old Testament had numerous ethnic affinities with their neighbors in and around Palestine (the area of Israel) and that the lines of ethnic demarcation were not hard and fast."[119] One scholar observes the following about the Shulammite, the wife represented in the Songs of Songs.

> It may seem like a small thing to us as modern
> readers but our heroine [the wife, the woman
> in the text] is the only woman in Scripture
> [and apparently only woman of color] who
> describes herself in her own words: 'I am

black and beautiful' (Songs 1:5). What a
mouth full! Unlike the matriarchs Leah and
Rachel, the Shulammite does not come to us
through the eyes of a male narrator (Genesis
29). Unlike Tamar, she is not forced to
disguise who she really is to avoid rejection
(Genesis 38). Unlike Ruth, she does not
apologize for being noticed, conspicuous,
or different (Ruth 2:10). The Shulammite is
unapologetic about who she is. She is black
and beautiful.[120]

Black and beautiful is like saying "dark and lovely," a
common expression used in today's Black community to describe
its sentiments about its people, particularly, their dark complexion.
Thus, it is likely that the wife in our text, and even the husband, were
people of color.

This couple's mutual love abounded. Unashamedly, the
wife avows in Songs 1:2 "for your love is more delightful than
wine." Her husband avows that "you have captured my heart with
one glance of your eyes... How delightful your love is my sister,
my bride. Your love is much better than wine..." (Songs 4:9-10).
Note that the "sister-bride designation here cannot in Israel refer to
sibling marriage; rather here it is simply an endearment expressing
the closest possible 'emotional' [not just sexual] tie."[121] Theirs
is a mutual love so strong and impenetrable that it could not be
perpetuated on sexual/romantic love alone. This couple of color
knew that love like this cannot be sustained by sharing a bottle of
wine over soft music. This Black man and woman had a marital love
so special and fulfilling, that "the Song of Songs gives us the only

picture of 'affectionate' love in the Old Testament ... The concept of one flesh, so eloquently illustrated in this book of scripture, is more than a sign, it is an expression of true marriage."[122] In his book, *God on Sex,* Daniel Akin notes that

> The word for love occurs repeatedly in Songs 1:2-7. A careful examination reveals love's connection to the mind, will, and emotions. Not only does love connect our intellect and our desires, but it also keeps them in proper balance… It is not just physical.[123]

This love, it should be noted, is apparent in and between Blacks in matrimony. Shulammite, the wife in the text of Songs 8:6-7, speaks with jubilation about the richness and strength of their love and about their longings being met.

> Set me as a seal on your heart, as a seal on your arm. For love is as strong as death; ardent love is as unrelenting as Sheol. Love's flames are fiery flames—the fiercest of all. Mighty waters cannot extinguish love; rivers cannot sweep it away. If a man [or woman] were to give all his wealth for love, it would be utterly scorned.

Theologians point out that "in ancient times, when few could write, one carried a seal suspended from the neck over the heart (Genesis 38:18, 25) or worn on the right hand (Jeremiah 22:24), with which to make his signature; hence the figure in the text."[124] Like modern day spouses sometimes do with tattoos, perhaps Shulammite was signaling to others that their inner love, their Black love, was robust and rewarding. The seal represented an outward, culturally recognizable symbol of their love for all to see. That visible, outward symbolism was to their love what water baptism represents to a new believer in Jesus: *deep connection*. Their interior love was solid. And it appears to have allied itself with an abiding sense of belonging.

Going further this wife said for them both, "I belong to my love and his desire is for me" (Songs 7:10). In *Strong's Exhaustive Concordance*, the Hebrew word for desire (*teshuwqah*) means "to stretch out or to run after—a longing."[125] This word is only found in two other scriptures: Genesis 3:16 and 4:7. "Whereas Genesis connects the woman's desire to her domination by the man, the Songs says desire is mutual."[126] Simply put, this Nubian couple longed to belong to each other and to their matrimony.

Their lavish, love-soaked longing was "repeated in part from Songs 2:16; 6:3... The married lovers and lovingly married Black couple are represented as separated [not by affection but location] with the girl [wife] longing for her beloved."[127] The greater the physical distance between them, the deeper their love. And the deeper their love, no distance could keep them apart. One Old Testament scholar states that "the girl [wife] wishes that she could always have her lover (husband) near her, like a brother, so that she could freely express her affection"[128] Solomon, the girl's husband, mirrored this deep affection.

There exists something striking about this married Black couple's experience. It underscores how important boundary building is for any serious couple out to protect their marriage.

> There is yet another symptom of the love
> sickness [more like love-healthiness] of [the
> couple] in the Song of Songs... The minor
> characters who figure in the song… all seem
> to serve the sole purpose of 'hindering and
> obstructing' the union of the lovers [spouses],
> and this is frequently accompanied by their
> inability to understand and appreciate the
> lovers' [spouses'] passion [affection] for
> each other.[129]

People outside a marriage can and often do create upheaval inside the relationship. Yet, the Songs nowhere suggest that these potential relationship "home wreckers" or antagonists were able to disrupt, much less destroy, the strength and sensitivity of this couple's abounding sense of belonging or love. This couple belonged to and not just believed in each other. They did so with a depth of husband-wife belonging that appears enhanced by an abiding sense of personal and interpersonal security. Security, a craving that is of the utmost urgency to most any Sista when it comes to her man, is another longing that growing couples must commit to nurture in their relationship.

We witness in the Song of Songs the kind of relational security that was personified not simply as lovers—but as friends. The wife overtly and publicly declares in Songs 5:16, "this is my love, and this is my 'friend', young women of Jerusalem." Her husband, Solomon, uses this of her in his native tongue in Songs 1:9, 15; 2:2, 10, 13; 4:1, 7; 5:2; 6:4.[130] In wisdom, this Brotha, Solomon, does for his wife what most every wife needs and asks of her husband. That is, verbally, regularly, affirming his sentiments about her. In so doing, a man asserts the emotional security and stability of the marriage itself. This is essential because a woman, more than the average man in marriage, needs to feel and hear such validation.

Shulammite's use of masculine key words in the text connotes a partnership, an association that was close and exclusive, not loose and casual.[131] This Nubian couple's friendship was closer than any set of brothers.

In Songs 5:10-16, we see "the bride moves on to describe other features of her lover's body, every one of which she finds exceedingly beautiful. Finally, to the 'girls' [daughters] in Jerusalem, she calls out: Such is my 'beloved', and such is my 'friend'".[132] The Sista-bride seems to be so secure emotionally that she can celebrate her husband's physique in descriptive detail to other women, but not without also celebrating his deep friendship and non-sexual association with her. Shulammite, scholars argue, was a young but secure woman and wife. The security in their relationship is often missing among couples young and old. Solomon and Shulammite provide a healthy, loving, realistic, and frankly, even sexy biblical model of Black marriage. In Proverbs 31, another loving pair models for Black married couples or engaged folk other core longings crucial to matrimonial bliss: an abiding sense of purpose, significance, and understanding.

A Black Marital Model of Purpose, Significance, and Understanding

The sage who penned Proverbs 31 helps us discern that "far from being mere chattel of the husband, the Hebrew wife here appears as the responsible head of the household."[133] Of course, a wife being head of household was far from likely in that day's culture. But her being portrayed in this light affirms the depth of her purposefulness. Moreover, a quite familiar reality in the world of most Black married couples is espoused in Proverbs 31:13-16, 23.

> "She [wife] selects wool and flax and works [purposefully] with willing hands. She is like the merchant ships, bringing her food from far away. She rises while it is still night and provides food for her household and portions for her servants. She evaluates a field and buys it; she plants a vineyard with her earnings… Her husband is known at the city gates, where he sits among the elders of the land."

Bible scholars substantiate that her husband was also a purposed man inside and outside of their marriage. "Because of his domestic security (provided by his wife), he could devote himself to matters (likely legal) of public concern."[134] The Proverbs here in realistic fashion parallel the unique historic and cultural reality of most Blacks having to balance marriage, core-longing care, and continuity, and the need for a two-income household. The wedded couple in Proverbs 31 demonstrates that with hard work, it is possible for Black spouses to strike a productive balance between cultivating a purposed life inside of marriage and one outside of marriage, all the while attending to each other's deep needs.

Equally useful to modern-day Blacks in their marriages is the sense of significance both spouses in Proverbs 31 seem to enjoy. This was more than domestic or professional importance. This couple also experienced spiritual and emotional meaning and understanding in and between each other.

Faith was a driving force in this marriage. "Her wealth, wisdom [understanding] and success are attributed to her faith. That is, the fear of God. She believes, like all true sages, that the beginning of wisdom is the belief in God as Creator and Sustainer. As a result, all the trappings of human desire that are noble are hers."[135] Author Robert Dentan says of the Proverbs 31 woman that her "physical beauty is not all that important (vs. 30); what is important is her intelligence, kindness (vss. 25-26), industry (vss. 15, 17, 27), and above all 'a religious spirit' (vs. 30)."[136] Her husband seems to reflect similar attributes, as detailed in verses 11, 23, and 28. Consequently, this God-fearing wife and husband duo enjoyed a mutual trust that would surpass many married couples today. Proverbs 31:11 says, "the heart of her husband 'trusts' in her." One Bible teacher asserts that "by viewing the wife, wisdom personified, from the husband's point of view, readers [individuals and couples] should be able to see that trust or security and understanding, is an exact outcome of wisdom."[137]

In the Hebrew language, trust (*batach)* here connotes both fact (security) and feeling (trust, assurance).[138] Mutual trust, along with other key intrinsic virtues like peace, patience, kindness, etc., is essential if any married couple is to advance and obtain a good marital outcome. The Song of Songs and Proverbs 31 are just two of many Biblical marriage metaphors. As it pertains to formational counseling and the aim to help Blacks succeed in marriage, one married Black sister, who is also a scholar, argues effectively on the benefit of marriage metaphors (stories) in scripture.

> The marriage metaphor mirrors the ways we, women and men, have wounded each other and have been wounded by interactions

marred by power, politics, and irrational expectations. All of this has left us deeply divided and bitter—estranged from, angry at, and suspicious of one another. For once, we might be able to admit, with the assistance of this metaphor, that part of our pain is the realization that, to our shame, hurting and being hurt have been always a part of what it has meant for us to live together as women and men. The marriage metaphor permits us to believe in the most unbelievable of all possible responses to our woundedness, namely, grace.[139]

These models of Black marriage echo the unique personal and/or societal forces that have influenced core longings for Black men and women in marriage in America. This spiritual and emotional maiming is something that the ministers and caregivers in formational counseling seek to combat by applying God's grace to wounded persons in marriage. Blacks who are married or engaged need to incorporate this Biblical concept as they attempt to attach their marriage to their core longings and to God in Christ. Jesus Himself cites it in Matthew 19:3-4, 7-8. "Some Pharisees approached Him [Jesus] to test Him. They asked is it lawful for a man to divorce his wife on any grounds? He [Jesus] told them . . . Moses permitted you to divorce your wives because of the hardness of your hearts. But it was not like that from the beginning." Hardness or softness of heart? As a spouse, you get to chose which you will operate in. But Jesus advocates only one of the two.

Jesus Summons A Softening of Affections in and Between Spouses

By softening, Jesus does not mean "mushy". He is, however, touting a God kind of agape affection in marriage that stokes unity, attachment, bonding, and resilience. In Matthew 19, the questioning of Jesus by the Pharisees was an attempt to entangle Jesus in a rabbinical debate over divorce and the Mosaic Law. They insisted that God *commanded* divorce in certain situations (Mt. 19:7).

Jesus countered by saying that God *allowed* it because of man's hardness of heart. In Matthew 19, the word hearts or (kardia in Greek) is a direct reference to a person's thoughts and feelings. "Hardness of heart" (sklerokardia in Greek) is the human attitude (personal and interpersonal) of resistance to or rebellion against God. It's a spiritual, relational, and emotional rupture or alienation from God existentially and between spouses in the marital context.[140] Jesus effectively advanced the debate from being a head (legal) discussion to being a heart (emotive/spiritual) discussion relative to matrimony.

Jesus was not out to reverse legal interpretation but rather to address "the hardness of heart."[141] The human heart is where spiritual and relational alienation between God and humankind starts and resides. Jesus was calling attention to the inner dysfunction that leads to emotional upheaval in married people. In focusing on the Mosaic law alone, the religious leaders were oblivious to the fact that God's love applied to the situation could change the hearts (and therefore the mindset and actions) of dysfunctional spouses, while the law merely identified dysfunctional behavior and prescribed punishment for it. Further, Jesus reminded the Pharisees that divorce wasn't in God's blueprint for marriage. The intention was for marriage to last a lifetime. A commentator on this verse of scripture in Matthew 19 said,

> From the standpoint of this radical attitude of Jesus toward the will of God, what is to be said of his position toward the Old Testament? Without contesting its authority, he makes critical distinctions among the demands of the Old Testament. Yes, Moses did permit divorce, but only 'in consideration of your hard-heartedness.' By no means is that the actual intention of God; rather He intends marriage to be inseparable.[142]

Jesus' aspirations for marriage and married people are also reflected in His comments found in Matthew 5:27-28, 19:1-10, and Mark 10:1-12. Homer A. Kent, Jr., says "since God's purpose called for man and wife to be one flesh, any disruption of marriage violates God's will."[143] The notion of disruption in marriage clearly includes core-longing wreckage as well. Jesus' definitive attitude was to summon the married culture in and outside of the church to a softening (tempering, moderating, healing) of hardened hearts.

Restoring or softening emotions, and defusing emotionally loaded issues, in and between Blacks in marriage (or any other people, married or single, for that matter) should therefore be the aim of the formational counselor or caregiver. The Bible has much to offer Blacks regarding marital coupling and core longings. The Bible also points us to the value of sound theology. For formational counselors and other Christ-centered caregivers, attempting to help Black couples grapple with their core-longing deficits, their theological motivation can be fastened on two concepts:

1. A theology of alienation fueling marriage.

2. A Black theology of liberation for Blacks in marriage

A Theology of Alienation Fueling Marriage

God Himself engraved a theological structure that would allow mankind to avoid or alleviate pain derived from aloneness or alienation. When God said in Genesis 2:18 "It is not good for man to be alone," it was a warning against the despairing and disconnected places of the heart. He knew the dysfunction that would come as a result of man being separated from fellowship with Him and with another being like him—namely, a woman as wife. And Lord knows, the COVID-19 pandemic not only exposed, but worsened, the despair brought on by alienation in and between spouses, and spouses-to-be.

In his work with Philip Roderick, Henry Nouwen characterizes the blight of pain born of relational alienation when he talks about transforming the loneliness stemming from such despair.

> If a human being is alone, in the sense that
> his uniqueness excludes him from entrance
> into every part of another person, there is
> a kind of separateness. It's fascinating and
> important to know that we constantly struggle
> to overcome that separateness, particularly
> because we feel that our aloneness quickly
> becomes loneliness. This is probably one
> of the greatest sufferings of our time – that

> people are lonely. In *marriage, there is a
> lot of loneliness*; in friendship, in intimate
> relationships, there's an enormous amount
> of loneliness, a sense of a yearning for
> communion. This is not satisfied, so enormous
> amounts of people suffer from loneliness
> – young people, older people. It is in the
> search arising from loneliness that people are
> looking for communion. They are looking for
> something to solve this pain.[144]

God's idea that man or woman not be "alone" reverberates deeply in the Black community. Even Nouwen's theological premise that "aloneness leading to loneliness" echoes more within the hearts and minds of Black men and women than for any other people. As a result, Black spouses often share the same physical space but not the same emotional space. They are separated emotionally, feeling alone and abandoned, with crippling loneliness.

The great news is the reversal from this marital negativity hinges not on Black married or engaged individuals, but rather on the truth that, "if God is a communion of persons inseparably related, then . . . it is in our relatedness to [not alienation from] others that our being human consist."[145] Thus, any isolation belief, behavior, and affections imposed on marriage is opposed to the God in Christ that many married Black couples revere.

Interestingly, Howard Thurman in his well-regarded work *Jesus and the Disinherited* holds that:

> A profound piece of surgery has to take
> place in the very psyche of the disinherited

[alienated] before the great claim of the religion of Jesus can be presented. The great stretches of barren places in the soul must be revitalized, brought to life, before they can be challenged.[146]

"Great stretches of barren places" existing in the souls of men and women is a reference to core-longing deficits or deep inner pain. However, I disagree with Thurman's call for profound action in the soul to occur before the great claim of Jesus can be presented to the person or into the situation. For me the great claim of Jesus is the gospel, grace, holiness, love, power, and Word of God through Christ Jesus, that enables any individual or life situation to be transformed. I am persuaded that it's because of the great claim of Jesus to the human experience, that the soul action to which Thurman refers is possible to wounded Blacks in marriage at any time. Those in marriages on emotional life support due to ruptured core longings can avail themselves to limitless possibilities when utilizing the claim of Jesus because all things are possible with God to those who believe.

One well-known catholic priest draws this conclusion about the gravity of the "barrenness of soul" ascribed to us by Thurman and personal/interpersonal alienation in and between people.

We are dealing with three levels of despair two of which are: in interpersonal relationships and in our church. That despair in personal relationships is becoming more and more visible. We feel disconnected. We search within our marriages, within our friendships .

> ..Anxiously, we look for a sense of belonging,
> rootedness, togetherness.[147]

This alienation, rooted in the neglect of core longings, if unrecognized and unaddressed, fuels destructive personal and interpersonal dilemmas. *In Theology of the Old Testament,* Edmond Jacob speaks on the Biblical ideal of marital unity and oneness.

> The most developed reflection of the unity of the married couple is in Yahweh's (God's) creation narrative from which we can extract the main contentions which the whole Old Testament makes on this subject. Since the woman is taken from man's body, she forms with him [or is supposed to] a single flesh; this is why man and wife unceasingly seek and call upon each other. The joy of reunion and the sadness of parting are celebrated in an incomparable way in the Song of Songs.[148]

What a cringe-worthy separation and celebratory reunion we witnessed of that brotha and sista, husband and wife, in the Song of Songs. When it comes to separation, it is argued by some that a marital break-up due to death is also a form of abandonment or aloneness leading to loneliness.[149] Studies suggest that because "relational" marital death is preventable, the pain is often worse than pain from a marriage partnership ended by death and typically longer lasting.

The late Michael Spencer, at one-time a Bible teacher, campus minister, and practical theologian of sorts known to hundreds of thousands of blog readers as the Internet Monk, talked and wrote on the pros and cons of aloneness.

> For Christians, being alone can have paradoxical outcomes. It can put you in closer touch with God, as Jesus modeled in his own life. But in the context of the church, being left alone, excluded, or isolated, can alienate you from other Christians and intensify your pain.[150]

As I have said repeatedly, the aim of this script and of formational counseling is to bring wounded people who are wed or engaged into close touch with God to help them deal with expressions of aloneness stemming from marital vows that have been breached and core longings that have been neglected.

Some theologians support a theology of solitude to recondition personal-spousal inner turmoil that accompanies aloneness or loneliness into private and sacred time with the Lord. Cultivating a healthy understanding, appreciation, and practice of solitude could be very therapeutic to the core-longing experience that Blacks face in marriage. Terry Wardle calls such solitude "'selective hiddenness.' This includes a healthy balance between biblical solitude and ongoing support from close friends and family. By solitude I [Wardle] mean extended periods of stillness that give space for God to speak."[151] This is an especially critical space for couples who cannot or are not speaking to each other.

Spencer calls a similar approach to solitude "'sacred individuality,' a sort of holy aloneness that cries out to be left alone with God. This… doesn't erase those parts of a Christian's experience that happens [or need happen] in the context of relationships, but this sacred solitude needs to be discovered, respected, and protected."[152] The psalmist put it like this, "be still and know that He is God" (Psalm 46:10). Formational counseling endorses encountering the presence of God through solitude. And solitude, among other spiritual disciplines, is crucial to the repair of ruptured core longings in spouses. To that end, Nouwen advised the following,

> There is so much loneliness, and many are sitting there complaining that they are forgotten by the world—*or their spouse.* They complain because interiorly they have no structures creatively to turn their solitude, their loneliness, into a gift for others for the world. Nouwen would further assert for couples that there is a theology of solitude that serves as a discipline in which you deal with your loneliness in such a way that it doesn't destroy you or others, but instead becomes a place to discover the truth of who you are [or need to become]. You are created by God who wants all your attention and who wants to give you all the love you need.[153]

A Bible-informed, Holy Spirit-inspired theology of solitude is another way of offering a sense of security and belonging to the soul. The security and belonging longed for by wounded Black spouses and sanctioned by God in Christ is a main component of the formational counselor's or caregiver's work. Thankfully, formational counseling is anchored in the premise of allowing Spirit-led surgery to take place within the barren places in the souls and psyches of any people. Spencer contends that a posture of solitude before the Holy Spirit is

> Where we most irrefutably hear God tell us that he loves us, and we come to know that no matter what other people may say about us or do to us, God will not abandon us. That holy solitude is the place where we find God's Spirit changing our affections and redirecting our identities. It is, for Jesus-followers [including spouses], holy ground.[154]

It's essential that Blacks, in or desiring marriage, find this holy ground and stand on it. In doing so, they will have their wounded affections and identities awash in the healing stream of the Spirit. Most Christ-centered theologians, pastors, ministers, counselors, caregivers, lay people, etc., likely accept that alienated people feel "uncared" for and need to be liberated from such angst. Remember, I believe, that the Word of God or Bible shapes and supports strong and sensible theology. Therefore, a second theological concept for the formational counselor or caregiver to consider is a Black theology of liberation for Black married couples who have core-longing deficits and feel uncared for.

A Black Theology of Liberation for Blacks in Marriage

Conceived by the National Committee of Black Churchmen in 1969, Black theology embodies the struggle for political, social, and economic justice between Blacks and Whites all within the scope of Jesus Christ.[155] However, Black theology critics, including myself, assert that Black theology's quest, fitting for its original time and place, is not suited in its current state to help Blacks combat today's range of paralyzing issues.

That's because Black theology's idea of liberation, to my disliking, is primarily aimed at facilitating a release of _racial_ bondage. For our aims, however, Black theology would also need to include an intentional striving for emotional/spiritual freedom for Blacks, especially for those in pain who are in or desire to be in marriage. My argument is that the aim of Black theology must be expanded to focus on Blacks and their relationships with each other, not merely Blacks' race and their racial tensions with others, namely, Whites. Bruce Fields makes the following observation regarding the Black community and its connection to Black theology.

> Many needs confront the African American community . . . Seemingly insurmountable problems such as _broken families_, promiscuity, teen pregnancy, drugs, gangs, rage, and hopelessness exist in desperate proportions. In order to be a viable force for the advancement of the African American community and to maintain its viability, _black theology_ must contribute to a resolution of these matters. It cannot exist as mere academic investigation and rhetoric.[156]

It appears Black theology was reincarnated in the year 2020-2021 through real time awareness, activism, and actions derived from a renewed robust public and private acknowledgement of the stronghold of systemic racism in America today. One area of focus is racism reflected in police brutality against Blacks. That said, if Black theology is to tackle the cultural realities that Blacks contend with nowadays, it should be open to addressing emotional, as well as racial, social, political, economic, and spiritual liberation.

Fields advances an evangelical critique of Black theology that I support. He says there are "four areas of black theology that must be continually evaluated for its liberation theme/posture: 1) its relationship to Christian tradition; 2) the question of hermeneutics [biblical]; 3) its relationship to the larger theological community; and 4) the danger of losing its Christian [Christ-oriented] identity."[157]

Additionally, Bradley asserts Black theology, in its current condition, is irrelevant because having the Black experience—not God in Christ—as its point of departure is wrong. My strong conviction is that God in Christ must be the point of departure for any theology. Otherwise, it is problematic and maybe even doomed to err and face eradication. Formational counseling could not agree more regarding the God in Christ primacy here. No wonder Bradley also advances five essential presuppositions he reasons Black theology needs to adopt in order "to be resurrected as a theology that is faithful both to the Scriptures and to the needs of black communities and churches [two key places where wounded blacks in marriages reside]."[158]

> 1) the absolute triune God as the starting point [relative to human suffering], 2) the absolute

primacy of biblical authority, 3) human dignity grounded in Imago Dei (the image of God, instead of race), 4) rediscovering a biblical doctrine of sin: personal and social, and 5) justice in line with the redemptive mission of God in Christ.[159]

I fully support these presuppositions because they are embedded in the Bible and embodied in the couple in our texts of Song of Songs and Proverbs 31. They are biblically endowed for any couple. I also fully support and identify with these presuppositions because they have linked me as care-receiver and caregiver in marriage to more than good theology, but to Life itself: *Jesus.* Formational counseling or a Christian caregiver's starting point is and always should be the Trinity: The Father, Son, and Holy Spirit. Black theology, aided by the Trinity, the Scriptures, empathic caregivers, and marital care-receivers, would be empowered to combat human suffering on a whole other level. It would require God's redemptive mission to materialize in the heart, mind, body, and relations of wounded people. And while each of their methods of ministry are different, both formational counseling and Black theology are or would be out to fundamentally "position or reposition" people for new, healthier encounters with God and humans. This might lead theologians, pastors, formational counselors, and other caregivers to advocate for, as I will now, the creation of a new theology undergirded by the Bible and vital tenets of the Christian faith that might be labeled: *Black formational counseling theology.* It would be a mixture of the best that formational counseling and a revamped Black theology can offer, in healing by liberating core-longing deficits in support of Black marriage.

Progress, Stability, and Hope Hinge-pin for Blacks in Marriage

Marriage has always been and is still very much a person-to-person partnering process and progress. Jesus said, "the two (individuals as spouses) shall become one." Few things are as personalized as marriage. Any two Black people in or determined to be married and needing help to get there, stay there, succeed there, or heal while there, will have to apply themselves *personally*. Personally to Jesus. Personally to the Word of God. Personally to sound theology backed by the Word of God. Personally to emotional growth and grooming. And if the need arises, personally to mental health support in the form of counseling, clergy, church, and a concentrated small group.

I have been married for thirty-four years. By the grace of God and by putting in the required relational work, my marriage is healthy. But this was not always the case, especially in the early years. Looking back, I can see the dysfunctional core-longing deficits and wounds that plagued me and my wife. At the outset of my marital journey I, like many married or engaged men, knew nothing of core longings, what caused or contributed to them, or how they impressed themselves on me as a person, as a man, and uniquely as a Black man. I definitely didn't know how to address them in me and the woman I married.

Arguably, understanding core longings and their fulfillment is what the Bible means by the statement in 1 Peter 3:7: "Husbands, dwell with your wife according to knowledge or understanding." For at least the first seven years of marriage, I felt pain and even caused pain. To be transparent, like so many men and women who set sail for the altar, I ventured into marriage with leftover and unresolved emotional issues that originated from childhood. All of this was intensified by my ignorance of the counseling and other forms of support available to help. As a result, we did what studies overwhelmingly show most married Black men and women do: we attempted to self-medicate our marital mess. Thanks be to God in Christ, we healed as individuals and spouses, and so did our marriage. But none of this healing happened before we both experienced a spiritual epiphany that led to a necessary reckoning with and remake of our roles in marriage. The section we will explore next may be lighter in tone compared to previous chapters, but not in substance.

I will espouse, along biblical grounds, "the heart of the matter" that is, the heart of Almighty God regarding marriage. It's my hope that these final three chapters will provide tangible application to all that has been said regarding Black marriage, with the intent of helping Blacks recover or protect their marriage option. The main hinge upon which the Black marriage option starts, stands, stays, and succeeds, is the heart of the matter of Almighty God.

Chapter 6

Black Men Seize to Relate Their Role in the Marriage Option

The most profound wisdom I can offer Black men concerning marriage is this: *it's bigger than you think, brother*.

It's Bigger Than You Think, Brother

A few months prior to getting married, I asked my father for advice. At that time, he and my mother had been married twenty-five of the forty years they would spend together before his death. In those days, it was not common for Black fathers and their sons to talk about such intimate subjects. Nevertheless, I mustered up enough courage to seek his advice by asking one question. "Daddy, is there anything you want to tell me now that I am about to get married?"

"Son, as a single man you can eat and break your plate. Not so once you get married."

My first thought, perhaps like yours, was what in the world does that mean? To be honest, it was years later before I understood the gravity of what Daddy meant. As a non-married man, you can basically do what you want. You can choose to stay single or date whoever will date you. When you're not married, you can play the field. I wouldn't advise you to do so. But like one old school hit song says, you may feel that's your prerogative. Man, you can decide to prolong the courtship for as long as possible in lieu of the marriage option or hurry to the altar. Or as a non-married man, you might even find yourself struggling to relate to and relay your role in the context of dating or courtship. But you can ill afford to live out these selfish antics in married life and expect to get away without serious marital damage. Why? Because matrimony is bigger than you think, brother.

Marriage is bigger than you think, brother, because marriage as God in Christ intended it is bigger than any man can imagine it. Whatever your view of the ideal marriage entails, it could never usurp what God in Christ has conceptualized for your union. Men, your marriage will never be more important to you than it is to God. You have to look at it through God's lens, for He has great love stored in marriage for you.

I'm reminded of an older Christian couple whom I'll call the Lees. Mr. Lee had been fighting cancer for some time. Being hospitalized and then convalescing in a nursing home during the COVID-19 pandemic had kept him from his wife of nearly seventy years. When I called to check on him at one point, he had been home for some time recuperating. Out of the blue he shared with me how his wife was demonstrating her deep love for him by her great care of him. She had become his caregiver because to her, he was a primary target of her love. He said to me, "Pastor, tell the men in our church how invaluable a wife's love is."

"When a woman falls in love it's nearly impossible to turn that thing off."[160] Those are the words of author and minister Renita Weems. Having been married nearly half the time as the Lees, I take Weems' assertion to be true. Women are natural nurturers. Take Eve, the first woman in Genesis 2. Her name means nurse or nurturer. This spirit of nurturing has been passed on to most every woman. Moreover, Mr. Lee's wife was modeling Jesus' admonition in John 13:34-35, "love you one another."

That said, it's not love from your wife that makes God's concept of marriage bigger than you think, brother. To the contrary, it's the love God has conceived of in Ephesians 5:25, the love of a husband toward his wife. Many husbands struggle to conceptualize this love, much less lavish it on their wives. Interestingly, it was a single brother (the apostle Paul), who wrote in that verse "husbands, love your wives, just as Christ loved the church and gave Himself for her."

That great love stored in you to be showered on your wife is no ordinary love. This says to me, and I hope to you also, that the Lord does not, my brother, expect your marriage to be an ordinary one. Your wedding might be ordinary by some standards. Perhaps in some ways your honeymoon the same, but your marriage need not be. And, no, the Lord here is not referring to a romantic or "falling in love" kind of love that brought you together with your spouse or fiancée. The love that Paul describes is far above that. This is a love that will "keep you and keep you two together" in ways and days you would otherwise deem impossible.

Christian psychologist, James Childerston, tells us studies suggest "men tend to confess to being in love sooner than women in a relationship."[161] But it's the "falling in love" kind of love that typically evaporates over time. Falling in love will need to transition into a deep companionate and continuity-giving love if the relationship is to survive and thrive. It must grow into a love that does not fizzle out at the first sign of trouble, but a love that is durable and still dynamic amid challenges because it is anchored in Christ's divinity and love.

Marriage is bigger than you think, brother, because it was ideated by God Himself, to alleviate your aloneness. The Creator God instituted marriage early on in His evolution of creation not only to perpetuate humankind's existence but also to uniquely enhance the human male and female's life. When God finished creating the world, He looked at all He had made and said it was very good (Genesis 1:31). Yet, in this perfect world, God pronounced to the male species of humankind, Adam, "it is not 'good' for man to be alone" (Genesis 2:18a). He said, "man" not "Adam," although the pronouncement included Adam. Truthfully, man has never been alone because God has always been there with and for him. But the male species has not always had the female to partner with in marriage until the Lord decided otherwise. God moved decisively, knowing a man's aloneness (separation, division), not from Him (God), but from someone like man himself (Eve) would lead to alienation and an absence of harmony and wholeness.

Now I must add that marriage is not, I repeat, is not for every man, nor for that matter every woman. To be frank, some people simply have no business being married. The Lord makes that abundantly clear in Matthew 19:1-12. But for every man for which marriage is intended, it was ideated by God to be used for more than just image, sex, children, or tax purposes. Marriage was originated to be an antidote vaccinating you from aloneness, alienation, and human absence that leads to streams of hurt.

Marriage is bigger than you think, brother, because it brings you into affiliation and alignment with someone "totally other" than you, yet "totally similar." The Lord God said to Adam (representing male kind) in Gen. 2:18b, "I will make a helper corresponding to him." That is, a woman, a wife that relates to and resembles the man (husband) but does not reflect the man in exactness. Alike but different emotionally, mentally, physically, sexually, neurologically, spiritually, and behaviorally.

These days, it's all too common to hear that "irreconcilable differences" brought divorce, separation, or defection to a union. But were you not already different, yet similar, at the start of the relationship? My wife and I were. We still are. But in marriage, difference does not have to lead to relational "indifference." How you lovingly, respectfully, and wisely, in God's strength, manage and massage the similarities and differences and move them from the "irreconcilable" to the "reconcilable" column will determine whether your marriage grows.

Marriage is bigger than you think, brother, because it can bless you with a unique intimacy you cannot experience on a higher plane with anyone else except God in Christ. Genesis 2:24 says, "this is why a man leaves his father and mother and bonds with his wife, and they become one flesh." By bond, the original language means "to impinge or to fasten, cleave, cling, to stick to, joining, to catch by pursuit, or to solder."[162] You get the idea: *togetherness*. Or, as I like to frame it: two-getherness.

I can hear some brothers saying, "that sounds too suffocating." God's goal for the marriage setting is never to smother you, but to foster deep relational sensitivity called intimacy or closeness between the two of you. Notice, fellas, the intimacy precedes the intercourse. In other words, God advocates here that your sensitivity comes before your sex activity. Love-matching before love-making. And if you still don't get it, let me use some Ebonics for you: "bond before getting busy."

Before you say the Bible's logic is outdated, you should know that it is consistent with behavioral science attachment theory. Daniel Siegel, a UCLA psychiatrist, describes attachment as "the sense of well-being that emerges from predictable and repeated experiences of care whereby people feel secure with another." This is necessary for most any relationship to feel secure, but especially those predisposed to a more inherent intimacy like parent-child, husband-wife. The operative phrase from Seigel's definition is "from predictable and repeated experiences of care." Brother, that is how you come upon intimacy (closeness) as a man to a fiancée or as a husband to a wife, and it's exactly as God said.

Upon closer scrutiny of Genesis 2:23-25, it's evident God expects married men, particularly those submitted to Him, to move from a family-level intimacy to a deeper and more exclusive matrimonial-level intimacy. Warning! This necessary emotional transition leading to attachment or bonding with your wife will require on your part a bit of divestment from your family of origin. Notice the Lord God says, "this is why a man leaves his father and mother and bonds with his (your) wife in Genesis 2:24a." The word leave does not mean you must abandon your relatives. But it does mean you'll have to loosen or relinquish some of your connectivity in healthy ways and repurpose it for you know who: your woman... your wife... your boo. It's a historical fact that thousands of ex-slave men and women, upon emancipation, went to seek their long-lost loves (spouses). And they were not even legally married. They were driven to this search, I am convinced, by a loving bond that only God could sanctify. I wish that for your matrimony, too.

Marriage is bigger than you think, brother, because it can sexually satisfy you without a search and without compromising your safety. Brothers, the heart of God orders that you get to not only be "one heart" but "one flesh" with the woman of your dreams in the marriage of your dreams. But here's something important: sex in marriage does not bring love, it affirms love. On the other hand, love in marriage brings sex... and a whole lot of it. I suspect you're feeling me, brother.

In Genesis 2:24c, "and they shall become one flesh," flesh here is a reference to the pudenda of a man or woman, or even nakedness."[163] The scriptures predate, yet validate the science of anatomy in its explanation of sexuality. It does so in its detailed description of the sexualized body, even pudenda, the sexual organs on the outside of a person's body we call genitalia. The pudenda nerve carries sensation from the external genitalia and skin of both sexes to other parts of the body. And when the sexual is coupled with the non-sexual, love making is intensely enjoyable to marriage partners. And you don't have to search for it or have grave safety concerns because its right in front of you all the time in your wife. You don't have to roam the streets looking for sex. Just mind the climate in your home and it'll find you in your wife. And it'll be satisfying, safe, and sacred.

Brother, what is God wanting you and me to grasp here regarding our roles in marriage? First, that it's a myth that marriage, especially once the children arrive, means the end of a fulfilling sex life. No, no! To the degree the non-sexual or emotional aspect of your marriage is flourishing, the sexual aspect will likely be fresh and frequent, barring physical limitations like erectile dysfunction (ED) for a male, endometriosis for a female, or unrealistic expectations, etc. From God's perspective in matrimony, a mattress and mating are not to be a mystery nor missing.

Second, you'll never impact your marital life and wife by applying yourself from the waist down, like you can from the waist up. Consistently seek to figure out how best to bond before getting busy so then you can get busy by bonding in the bedroom. In doing so, you block out room for an affair or divorce prospect to overrun your nuptials.

Marriage is bigger than you think, brother, because it's so big in God's eyes that He hates its alternative: Divorce. I said divorce. Not divorcees, but divorce. It seems everybody has an opinion on marriage these days. Why should I get engaged or married? Why should I not do so? How long should I wait to get married? How long should my engagement period be? Is marrying necessary if I can achieve what I want by dating? But have you thought to ask, Lord, what is your stance on marriage relative to divorce? His stance is simple. Straightforward. Substantive. He "hates" divorce (Malachi 2:14). He "honors" marriage (Hebrews 12:4).

Neither the Lord nor me are naïve when it comes to divorce. It happens. And frankly, for good reason at times. And as we have said, He sanctions those legit but limited reasons. However, it doesn't erase His distaste for divorce. On the flip side, marriage happens for not-so-good reasons at times. Nevertheless, the Lord has an extremely high view of marriage. He holds the totally opposite view of divorce—again never divorcees.

The takeaway for you, brother, is this. You nor I will ever think, feel, or act more highly or honorably on behalf of our marriage than God. And guess what, whether your marriage is in poor or phenomenal shape, He thinks, feels, and is poised to act the same to help a brother out. And no one will move with more dedication to dissuade divorce for you than Him. That helps explain why many God-fearing people have survived and gone on to thrive in marriage after experiencing some of the worst marital ordeals you can imagine. I can testify that in my darkest hour, while staring the idea of divorce in the face, He kept me (us) from it. While we are not slaves, I think we can and should glean from our ancestors' resolve amid extreme hard times to keep divorce out of our mouths and out of our marriages.

Marriage is bigger than you think, brother, because aside from God, marriage will likely pose your greatest "love challenge." If you had problems or challenges loving people before entering married life, marriage will either magnify or help modify your love ethic. In Ephesians 5:25, God says, "husbands, love your wives, just as Christ loved the church and gave himself for her to make her holy, cleansing her with the washing of water by the word." The Lord literally commands you *"to love your wife as if you were God Himself loving her."* There is hardly any way to misread that command. Of course, you are not Jesus! Yet you're commanded to love your wife as if you were. And you can love her like this only with Jesus' love funneled through you.

Marriage is bigger than you think, brother, because you cannot simply "think" your way to it or "through it." You'll have to emote and that right deeply. Many men tend to misinterpret emotional love as mushiness. Call it what you will but you'll hardly be able to escape the need to display emotions in marriage. For the duration of your marriage, brother, your wife needs and deserves emotional engagement with you. But it must be genuine.

Return with me to the book of origins (Genesis) for insight. Genesis 2:22-23 says, "then the Lord God made the rib he had taken from the man into a woman and brought her to the man. And the man said: This one, at last, is bone of my bone and flesh of my flesh; this one will be called woman, for she was taken from man."

I jokingly say that once God "brought, presented or gave" Eve to Adam, he was so excited and emotional that he sounded like the famous singer, Etta James, when he said "this one, at last..." Adam knew his lonely and single days were done. Furthermore, Adam took genuine initiative, because without being asked by God or his wife, he verbalized and displayed his emotions with enthusiasm. He saw her for who she truly was. He recognized, respected, and related to Eve's uniqueness. He voiced his feelings for her deeply, without resorting to sex in some attempt to either conceal or convey his emotions, or somehow exploit hers.

Don't get me wrong. I imagine that in the mix of all his deep emotional connecting, Adam did squeeze and hold his wife to convey his heart. Most men do, especially when she is new to him. Brothers, I encourage you to use Adam's techniques. Don't try to mimic the pretend romantic overtures of Billy Dee Williams, Idris Elba, or Shemar Moore. Instead, learn to connect with and to your wife in healthy ways that promote emotional bonding. Do this genuinely, uniquely, and continuously.

None of Adam's emotive methods drew the Lord's disapproval. I certainly hope you emote well and that your efficiency is affirmed by your spouse. But like most anything in marriage, this too is a work in progress

Marriage is bigger than you think, brother, because to make it successful, you have to figure out how to promote unity over individuality, without losing yourself and while valuing your spouse's individuality. Taking a cue from the French novelist Francoise Sagan, Tim Keller, says "love is the most liberating freedom-loss of all."[164] He said it's the most *liberating* loss of freedom, not the most *limiting*. Marital love fits this description. In Mark 10 and Matthew 19, Jesus put it this way: "the two shall become one." That is, two individuals morph into one whole team—not one whole individual.

Most people would not associate freedom loss with liberation. You should and must with marriage. In matrimony, independence should be replaced by interdependence. All for one—one for all. Keller says

> "For a love relationship to be healthy there must a mutual loss of independence. It cannot be just one way. Both sides must say to the other, I'll adjust to you. I'll change for you. I'll serve you even though it means a sacrifice for me. If only one party does all the sacrificing and giving, and the other does all the ordering and taking, the relationship will be exploitative and will oppress and distort the lives (and the love) of both people."[165]

My wife would even make the case, and I agree, that we cannot assume that the giving and receiving is always 50-50. Truthfully sometimes its 80-20, 70-30, etc. Honestly, I'm not sure marriage is ever 50-50. And when you look at it through the lens of Christ and how you as a man are expected to love your wife, it should leave you, me, and other husbands asking, "should it be?!" Considering the love, joy, support, partnership, spiritual blessing from God, the accompanying sex, offspring, family, communal impact, and so on you receive, you should hardly feel any notion of your marriage being a "limiting freedom-loss." If you do so over a long period, my brother, it is highly likely you and/or your wife are living in neglect of your individual and corporate core longings care.

Marriage is bigger than you think, brother, because you will likely need help at times "thinking through" its challenges. Of all the marital couples I have interacted with in my life, they all have one thing in common: *challenges*. The challenges won't always emanate from inside your marriage. They may originate from outside as well. Either way, I hope you'll seek help when you discern that you are in over your head. I'll admit from my personal and professional experience, men as husbands tend to seek help last. Dead last. Not first, like their wives tend toward. Given what we have highlighted thus far what, if any, area would you acknowledge you need help with? Either in preparation for marriage or in your marriage right now. There is no cause to be ashamed in asking for help. Challenges can work to your benefit and growth in the process of you and your wife becoming one. When you face difficulties as a couple, it's the time to be assured or reassured as to what direction you're traveling on your matrimonial map. An opportunity to make course corrections, if need be.

In previous segments, we saw that our African American slave and ex-slave ancestors sought civil help, church help, and communal help. More to their credit, they sought help from the Source exceedingly beyond all those put together: *God in Christ.* Because of our ancestors' efforts, help is more readily available to you and me than they could ever have dreamed of, in the form of professional counseling, marriage intensives, conferences, articles, books, etc. For the sake of your marriage, don't be like Adam, who when his life, including his marriage, was troubled, opted to hide instead of seek help—even eluding God's help (Genesis 3:8-12).

Help brings hope. Hope leads to healing. Healing leads to something no man as a husband in his right mind wants to forego: *Respect.* Women, as wives, respect a husband who is willing to seek help.

Finally, marriage is bigger than you think, brother, because it is one of the greatest sources of "respect" you'll ever be privy to. Men fight all day, everyday, on the streets for respect. This truth is quite acute for Black men. You shouldn't have to fight for it in your home within the context of marriage. Of course, you do have to vie for self-respect within culture at times. But chances are high that if you apply yourself to what we have presented, you'll rarely have to vie for respect as a husband from your wife. It'll be lavished on you by your wife as a beautiful byproduct of your marriage. As you learn to love your wife as Christ loves the church, she, in turn, will be provoked to respect you. By marital respect, wife to husband, Ephesians 5:33 means for her to exhibit a sense of awe. This awe is short for awesome, not "aw shucks" toward you. You're not God, but you're God's man for her, and for that, you're to be viewed and handled as awesome by your wife.

Former pastor, Rev. Dr. Emerson Eggerichs in his book *Love and Respect* uses the acronym CHAIRS to communicate what men expect this respect to look like.

C – Conquests. Meaning your wife will respect your desire to work and achieve, not to be a workaholic and overachiever.

H – Hierarchy. Meaning your wife will respect your desire to protect and provide.

A – Authority. Meaning your wife will respect your desire to serve and to lead. Not in some perverted patriarchal way, but in a way consistent with a relevant understanding of your God-given role as we have outlined and through relating to God.

I – Insight. Meaning your wife will respect your desire to analyze and counsel. Of course, it's wise, quite wise, that you discern when your wife needs these two tools from you and when she needs your listening ear or holding arms.

R – Relationship. Meaning your wife will respect your desire for shoulder-to-shoulder friendship with her and others. For example, she will watch or attend a ballgame with you because she knows this is a favorite pastime of yours. Or she will not be intimidated or jealous of you doing so with your guy buddies or family from time to time.

S – Sexuality. Meaning your wife will respect your need for sexual intimacy. This also implies she will respect and recognize that without sex, you'll tend to be a bit of a wreck.[166]

As you sit in these CHAIRS, brother, you'll be able to be seated any place in your house feeling a strong sense of respect. If you'll accept and incorporate the concepts laid out in this chapter aimed at giving clear definition to your job as husband, you'll relate to and relay your role well to the one who needs it most: your wife.

Chapter 7

Black Women Seek to Relate Their Role in the Marriage Option

The reigning emotion most wives desire to have fulfilled is love. As you seize how best to relate as a Black married woman, you'll discover that marriage demands more sensitivity than you might feel.

It's More Sensitive Than You Feel, Sista

Rev. Dr. Emerson Eggerich uses the acronym COUPLE to explain the love women want from their husbands.

C – Closeness. Meaning your husband values that you want to be close to him though not to the point where he, or both of you feel suffocated.

O – Openness. Meaning your husband wants to open up to you, not due to or in the heat of the moment, but from the warmth of the relationship.

U – Understanding. Meaning your husband doesn't automatically try to "fix" you or all the problems. Rather, he listens to gather understanding. To phrase it differently, as James 1:19 says, you desire him to "be quick to hear (attentive listener), slow to speak (before speaking), and slow to anger (blow up)."

P- Peacemaking. Meaning your husband values the importance of saying "I'm sorry." To do that requires, humility, regret, repentance, and a desire for reconciliation.

L – Loyalty. Meaning your husband is committed to you as your lover, provider, protector, etc.

E – Esteem. Meaning your husband honors and cherishes you above all other women. His momma and birth sisters may run a close second, but you'll come first.[167] However, it'll take more than you, Sista, giving or receiving love to gain, retain, and maintain your marriage. One major requirement on your part will be R.E.S.P.E.C.T. Respect is a derivative of belonging, in this case, his sense of belonging to you, his bride, in marriage. You can give your husband something black men in America have enjoyed little of: R.E.S.P.E.C.T.

Respect is paramount. Yet for some reason it's easier for a wife to give love than respect. Yet, learning how to respect your man as your husband is godly and biblical. Ephesians 5:33 says, "the wife is to respect her husband." Respect has huge personal and interpersonal ramifications for your marriage. For his part, the man must do the work to earn the respect his wife gives him. Sista, please hear me! Your respect is not to be blind loyalty by any means. Rather, it's that sense of awe spoken of in the previous chapter. It's viewing and handling him as awesome.

And just so you grasp the enormity of what God intends, the enormity of what respect engenders to your husband, and the enormity of your responsibility in this area of marriage, take into consideration Shaunti Feldhan's research. Shaunti surveyed thousands of men on marriage and relayed her results in a book entitled *For Women Only, a* book for single, engaged, or married women about men. Surveying some three thousand plus men, she asked the following question: "Which is most important to you in marriage, your wife's love or respect?" Sista, the answer overwhelmingly was respect.[168] It's not that he doesn't want or need your love. Of course, he does! However, he wants and needs your respect more. Respect settles a husband like love secures a wife in marriage.

One additional way you can display respect is by helping him. Not by helping him "be" but by assisting the life you two share to be lived. It is called being a mate that helps. *A helpmate.*

I know it's not sexy sounding, it's sound. I think this helpmate concept resonated more with married folk in the slave and ex-slave and Jim Crow era. This world of our African American ancestors was so based on grunt work that it required a pooling of resources that proved and pruned the love and respect between spouses. Let me go back even further. It was in the perfect environment, a paradise, that the man discovered he needed a helpmate. How much more is this true in the imperfect world in which we live? The need for this relational reality was revealed in Genesis 2:20 when it says, "the man gave names to all the livestock, to the birds of the sky, and to every wild animal; but for the man no *helper* was found corresponding to him." Sista, within the confines of marriage, you're that helpmate or corresponding helper. Not his momma, boss lady, sisters, daughter, or his friends who are girls. This position is reserved solely for one girl—you, his wife.

By helpmate or corresponding helper, it's meant you're to aid, not arm, your husband to protect the life you two set out to build. He's responsible to arm himself to aid and provide protection to the whole process and journey. The best way I know for you as wife to get at this is to allow God to show you how to aid your husband. No other woman is expected by God, nor should be expected by you or your husband, to execute this role. In other words, you're to work with—not for—your husband in matrimony, as he takes the leading role, which is to love and lead you in marriage as if he were Jesus Himself doing both.

The specifics of how you go about being a helpmate providing aid to your husband differs from couple to couple. However, you should expect to have to do so in a few non-negotiable areas, i.e., helping your husband with *finances, fathering, and fostering understanding of you.*

Since Blacks' arrival in America, Black women have always had to help Black men carry the financial load. It's still true of Black spouses in America today. They even do it as girlfriends or live-in partners routinely today. Rarely have Black couples been able to survive or thrive as a one-income-earner pair. We cited this about the couple in Proverbs 31. The wife in the text was quite industrious, entrepreneurial-like. And I'm sure it proved to be an enormous blessing to the family. Now, I'm not suggesting you need to be an entrepreneur, Sista. Not at all. But you'll most likely need to help finesse the finances in some tangible way. Perhaps even as a breadwinner. Perhaps as a non-breadwinner. Perhaps as a housewife, not likely with today's economic pressures but not impossible. Perhaps as the family's CFO, Chief Financial Officer, in-charge of managing the household budget and dispensing with the bills.

Perhaps partnering with your husband to build a business. Perhaps holding your husband and yourself fiscally accountable. Either way, every day, he'll need your financial assistance.

Sista, your husband will even need your help fathering. I suspect this notion might have you scratching your head. But here is what I mean. I'm not referring to getting pregnant. That's a given. I also don't mean you replacing or usurping his role as father. Nor do I mean you instructing him on how to be a father. But there is much you as a woman and mother can and will need to do to aid his fathering role, especially in the areas of *devotion, discipline, and distancing.* Your husband as father should honor the biblical admonition in Ephesians 6:4, "fathers, don't stir up anger in your children, but bring them up in the training and instruction of the Lord." You, Sista, can help him not reject but raise the kiddos right and with great results.

Devotion as a father implies emotion as a father. Your husband's fatherhood cannot be detached from healthy emotion. However, he should steer clear of toxic emotions the Bible warns against, like anger. In Ephesians, anger literally means to be "enraged" or polluted by poisonous anger aimed toward the children. A father's devotion and healthy mental state prevents him from pushing the kids away or potentially bringing ruin to their upbringing, thereby losing them or causing separation. Most women have a God-given capacity to nurture offspring (unless this gifted capacity has been mitigated or maligned by abuse). Who better to help a brother out when it comes to his parenting role than you, Sista? Another very experienced father, grandfather, or child expert can offer him wisdom, but no one will have more access and interaction, thus opportunities to influence his fathering, than you. Finger pointing from you or inducing blame and shame won't work.

However, helping your husband become cognizant of his approach, affections, or actions in his fathering will enhance the effectiveness of his fatherhood. Help him to become cognizant of his child/children's responses, reactions, and emotional/behavioral regard for his fathering techniques.

This aids his discipline and distancing practices. Even the best of fathers can be "overbearing" when it comes to disciplining their children. Some can even be "overindulgent" when it comes to doing for them. I would argue African American fathers are more prone to being "overbearing" with their kids because of the external pressures applied on us from society, as discussed in previous chapters. Your sense of nurturance can help him strike a balance between being overbearing and overindulgent when it comes to discipline.

Your helpful insight will be especially appreciated when your husband, as a father, finds himself angry with his child or children like Ephesians 6:4 describes. That is, angry with a "passionate ire, rageful, wrathful, exasperated, vengefully punitive or violator, breaker, or transgressor-type" anger.[169] Things are likely not going to end well when a person issues discipline with uncontrolled anger. Indeed, children need help in the form of discipline from time to time to break bad habits. But what children don't need is the breaking, the violation or transgressing of their spirit through faulty or overbearing discipline. We call that parental negligence or abuse. While your husband, as a father, is responsible for arming himself against such an approach, Sista, your support is vital. Talk with him, walk, pray, stand strong, and trust God to move him off the cliff.

Without healthy devotion and discipline protocols, the distance between a father and the children may balloon to become a negative factor. Relations between fathers and children fare best when the parties are together emotionally, spiritually, and physically. Gary Chapman in his well-known work *The Five Love Languages* says one-way kids spell love is T.I.M.E.[170] This is especially true when kids are young. If your kids are young, enjoy the time you have with them now. Once they become adults, you'll have nowhere near the time with them as you do now. In fact, you and your husband may find you'll often have to negotiate for the time you have with them as adults. But if I had to translate the word "time" into an acronym to convey how important adolescents and adult kids think time spent with a father is, it would be the following.

T – Time

I – In

M - My father's "undivided" presence is

E – Exhilarating and especially needful.

Young kids cannot explain that, but they feel that way. Adult kids feel that way but may not articulate this need to their father. Sista, you may have to help bridge the gap.

Your husband as a father may falsely believe his ability to provide for his kids defines the overarching nature and scope of his fatherhood. He may feel it's primarily your role as his wife and their mother to deliver the parental emotional connection the children need. He may not carve out time for the kids due to his work demands and priorities. On the other hand, he may be willing to provide the time connecting to the kids, but he may not possess the temperament to do so when present. As we saw with discipline, time without the proper temperament may damage the heart and mind of an adolescent or adult child. And God forbid he would play favorites.

Take for instance, my father and I. Unlike him and his father, he and I shared no mechanical affinity whatsoever. My father was a gifted mechanic. His father had gifted use of his hands in other ways. I had no interest in being so! Thankfully and to his credit, Daddy never held it against me. He knew I wasn't the outdoors/mechanical type. I was more the bookish-type and quiet like a guy named Jacob in the Bible. The difference between me and Jacob is that his father loved his older brother Esau and not Jacob because Esau was a skilled hunter, something their father valued. Since Jacob preferred quiet/constructive time in the house and didn't hunt, his father didn't hold him "in his heart" as he did Esau. Favoritism like this is toxic to family dynamics. I'm so grateful to God that my four siblings and I didn't have to deal with that under our father's hand.

Any persistent pattern like this is likely to result in emotional and/or physical dissension between father and kid(s). Worse yet, it can negatively serve to influence a child's image of the loving Heavenly Father. While you as wife and mother cannot be expected to resolve all the potential pitfalls in your husband's fathering, there are some steps you can take to relieve these issues. Ideally, your husband as a father will leave his children experiencing little to no residue of the troublesome factors mentioned. But even if he's a fantastic father, who is deeply devoted and takes a decisive yet discerning approach to discipline, your husband will need to draw on your nurturance and instinctive skill from time to time. Don't be surprised if you find you must help him keep his work and family obligations balanced, or his disciplinary methods fair. His need of your support here will certainly be true if he holds a very demanding job or travels a lot in his profession. Unless he is an extrovert and loves gatherings, your husband will likely require your help rallying the family together for shared events. While most introverted dads deeply love their kids, don't be alarmed if your husband commands an extra nudge to spend the time with them. I know I do as an introvert sometimes. Okay, well, more than sometimes. But I haven't once regretted the outcome from my wife occasionally urging me to spend the T.I.M.E. with my sons and their families, nor will your husband. And please don't get me started on spending time with those grandbabies... pure joy!

One area you might not consider when you think of being a helpmate is the necessity for you to foster your husband's or future husband's understanding of you, as his wife. Besides God, there is no better person he can learn from. Some men wrongly believe they know women. Some men rightly believe they understand women. Your husband, however, unlike any other man, has the God-given responsibility to "live (dwell/interact) with his wife according to understanding (1 Peter 3:7)." Not according to sex, kids, money, work, in-laws, etc., but insight or knowledge. I can tell you that marriage is no place for guessing games or widespread speculation between spouses. And while your hubby has his own responsibility to strive to realize who you are, there is much you can do in the way of disclosure to further his awareness of you as his wife. Most wives want their husband to recognize, accept, and connect deeply with her through her likes and dislikes, pains and perplexities, secrets and sayings, whims and wants, flaws and laws, limits of herself and of him (husband), and her strengths and weaknesses. She wants to know that her husband *gets her and gets how to go about fulfilling her needs as his wife for life in Christ.* I'm advocating for "need-based" awareness not "want-based." Without need-based awareness, the relationship bleeds in pain, brokenness, and confusion.

Sista, help your husband explore the core longings we discussed earlier. It might be uncomfortable, unfamiliar territory for him and you at first. But it's worth the investment. Help him become an expert at which of the six core longings (inner needs) are most important to you. Is it an abiding sense of belonging, love, purpose, security, significance, or understanding that you long for, or perhaps some combination of these? Like a curious, observant scientist in a lab, explore with your husband how best he can go about fulfilling your core longings. One marriage expert equates fulfilling someone's inner needs with speaking their "love language."[171] I call it the "grunt work" of love. Call it what you wish, you can and must help your husband "love you as Christ loves the church." As you open yourself up for examination and exploration, and he wisely opts to enter in to search your heart, head, and actions for understanding, he'll be empowered to not undermine his husbandly response to your wife-needs. And he'll likely reciprocate by opening up to you about his core longings. By the way, the Lord makes an even deeper first century claim on expressive love in 1 Corinthians 13:1-8, for any husband or wife to glean from and practice in wedded union.

Another topic that may prove to be a challenge for you to relate to and convey to your husband in marriage is: *your inner beauty versus your outer body image*. Beauty and body image to any woman is a touchy issue. But to Black women, it carries a hypersensitivity and may even be a source of emotional trauma. Unfortunately, this has been the case for Black American women since slavery. As I write this, there are African and African American women, young and old, attempting to dye their skin a lighter shade. To this day, it's a well-documented fact that slave and ex-slave women were labeled nigger-women, wenches, darkies, apes, gorillas, and the list of derogatory names go on and on. Black men folk didn't fare any better. How did our female ancestors survive and thrive with some semblance of dignity under such horrific scrutiny of their self-image, the Black body, and their inner being?

To this day, all types of Black women, unlike Black men, struggle with the issue of colorism. Spike Lee in his 1980s movie *School Daze* depicted this struggle that has been occurring on American soil since the early seventeenth century. For instance, it's believed Frederick Douglas's first wife of forty-four years, a black woman named Anna Murray Douglas, was not fully accepted by those in their circle, which included some abolitionists. However, his second wife of eleven years, Helen Pitts Douglas, was accepted. Why? Because she was white. The first wife wasn't thought of as being "pretty enough" for their societal circles, given she was a dark-skinned Black woman.

The question of being "black and beautiful, dark and lovely" isn't nearly as much a source of shame for most brothers. Being black and strong and dark and dynamic, yes! But not the former. This black and beautiful stigma plaguing Black women can even be seen or measured in cosmetics. In their powerful book entitled *Shifting: The Double Lives of Black Women in America,* Charisse Jones and Kumea Shorter-Gooden, citing *Business and Industry* and *PR Newswire,* tell us "as a group, Black women spend three to four times more on cosmetics and beauty products than White women, a huge difference accounted for in part by the lily complex.[172] The lily complex is the attempt by black women to alter, disguise, and cover up their physical self to assimilate and be accepted as attractive to meet the mainstream ideal set by non-blacks.[173]

Darlene Clark Hine and Kathleen Thompson cite another striking point about Black women and beauty products acknowledging "it is significant that the first woman in the United States to become a self-made millionaire was Madame C.J. Walker, an African American woman who developed and sold personal hair care products, including the hot comb, which is used to straighten hair."[174] It appears many Black women opt to buy beauty to comply or compete with someone else's concept of beauty. In addition to being dismayed by what all of that infers, I'm sitting here wondering where Black women get the money that enables them to spend "three or four times more on cosmetics and beauty products than white women."

I believe the lily complex can be reversed, and the threat it poses to your soul and married life can be minimized. The lily complex is a derivative of the Sisterella syndrome, Sisterella being the ebonized version of Cinderella. You know the story of Cinderella and how she was mistreated and maligned by her stepmother and stepsisters, no matter what she did to try to appease them. The Sisterella syndrome is defined "as being the Black woman who honors others but denies herself. She achieves in her own right—indeed, she may overachieve—yet she works tirelessly, sometimes masochistically, to promote, protect, and appease others. She is trying so hard to be what others want and need that she has lost control of the shifting process. It's overtaken her. Sisterella has had to give too much to others. Or she's given up too much of herself. She has so internalized society's messages that say she is less capable, less valuable, that she has stopped trying to prove otherwise. She has lost sight of her own gifts as well as her own needs. Her identity is confused, her personal goals are deeply buried, and she shrinks inwardly. She becomes depressed, sometimes severely so."[175]

As I see it, regarding the lily complex, she tries to "look the part," without falling apart, to facilitate being aligned with something she was not born into. And "looking the part" often means to look "white." My Sista, some people call that the lily complex, but I call it the "lowly complex" because this stuff can and has brought many a Black woman (and sometimes the Black man she loves and who wants to love her) *mighty low*.

The two inquiries I posed earlier need to be answered in hopes of steering you clear, as a wife or future wife, from bringing these negative stigmas onto yourself and into married life. The first question was: *how did our female ancestors survive and thrive in marriage with some semblance of dignity living under such horrific scrutiny of their self-image of their Black body?* The second question was: *how can society, your husband, and particularly you, Sista, help reverse the threat or impact of the lily complex on your soul and in the process posture you to be stronger for marital life?* The answer comes from the Lord God, who made you as you are. Although it's quite in vogue among women now, you can ill afford to relate to or relay your marital role of a wife via beauty standards, and certainly not via distorted ones.

The remedy not only comes from the Utmost Source, but it was translated through a married man. His name was Peter. In 1 Peter 3:3-5, he says to women, "don't let your beauty consist of outward things like elaborate hairstyles and wearing gold jewelry, but rather what is inside the heart—the imperishable quality of a gentle and quiet spirit, which is of great worth in God's sight. For in the past, the holy women who put their hope in God also adorned themselves in this way, submitting to their own husbands." Sista, this protective directive may be old, but its efficacy is as good as ever as it concerns how you handle self-image, self-esteem, self-actualization, and self-management of your beauty-body-blackness consciousness. As you apply this passage of scripture to your life, it takes the emphasis off society's influence and view of your Black beauty and body, and places it in a much safer, succinct, sacred, spousal, and even money saving place for you. With this approach, you, your spouse, and God in Christ, your God I pray, are eager to see you only seek to have your appearance please a loving, supportive, audience of three: *Sovereign God, spouse, and self.* As for society, well, who cares? God does not, and neither should you or your husband. The Lord is vastly more concerned with "what is inside the heart – the imperishable quality of a gentle and quiet spirit, which is of great worth in God's sight." He advocates, promotes, commands, instructs, empowers, and encourages this personal development and management specific to women throughout the scriptures, not just in our chosen text of 1 Peter 3. As for the outer appearance, the Bible says women are to "dress in moderation." I suppose if you, Sista, identified the most liberal and most conservative dressers you know, then, dressed yourself midway in style betwixt the two, you'd likely not only please but honor God, your husband, and yourself. And you'll dethrone any societal pressures to conform otherwise.

Note the incentive and blessings attached to prioritizing the nourishing of your inner being over and above your outer body: 1) Your inner being unto God becomes of "an imperishable quality— and of great worth in God's sight." Even on your best day, you cannot garner "imperishability" or "such worth" with your looks. 2) Your inner being, when nourished in the Lord, becomes "gentle and quiet—but strong," and thus is empowered to help you keep your outer being from languishing under the rigid and quixotic beauty demands from others, 3) Your inner being will empower you to not "let your beauty consist of outward things like elaborate hairstyles and wearing gold jewelry or fine clothes." Now to be clear, Sista, this isn't a biblical/spiritual license to "let yourself go!" Few husbands would appreciate that. Not even God welcomes that because your body "is the temple of the Holy Spirit" (1 Corinthians 6:18)—and your heart the epicenter of it. Your beauty should radiate from what's inside your heart, character, and spirit. Outer beauty should complement, but never compromise or replace inner beauty. 4) Your inner beauty focus will bring you more fully into surrender and alignment with your marital mission with and to your husband. Adorning your body to God's fashion standards will strengthen your matrimony because once married, Sista, per God, your body is no longer exclusively your own where your husband is concerned. The reverse is equally true (1 Corinthians 7:1-5). But your husband will not likely be preoccupied with beauty-body-blackness image like you may be. Thus, he can and should help keep the lily complex at bay in the marital space. It also seems wise that any Christ-honoring, God-fearing, or down-to-earth, Sista, would want and work to present and protect her body-beauty-blackness image (from the lily complex) in this way, especially given this age of body (outward appearance) focus in which we live.

If need be, some of this will require behavioral change(s) on your part. Marriage often exacts necessary change in our actions. And hardly nowhere should modest behavior be more valued than with a woman as a wife. Ahead of being a mother, being a wife is the most important role you can have. Your daily habits will be a clear indication that preservation of your marriage option is often more sensitive than you feel, Sista. Most of our ancestors' post-Civil War marriages enjoyed longevity because they embraced this. But please, Sistas or brothers, do not interpret this as a summons for her to be a "bionic or superwoman" in marriage. That would be unwise and unfair to her and out of step with God's purpose for her in matrimony. Furthermore, Sistas do not need any more undue burden placed on them than they feel they already carry. And having to bear others' misguided expectations, while tending to their own behavior, is not baggage our Sistas as wives need.

And what is more, personal conduct, like thoughts and emotions, is influenced by beliefs. Husbands and wives cannot function in their role in fruitful ways if they're operating under false, anti-intimacy, or limiting attitudes that distort behavior. What follows are some other essential principles you must or must not foster as a wife. To get at this we need, to return to Proverbs where we found one of the biblical couples who models marriage and its benefits for us.

Belief #1: Sista, you must believe that respecting your husband's need for respect is critical, given he is a man and given the Black male's chronic "belonging" issue in America. Proverbs 12:4 says, "A wife of noble character is her husband's crown, but a wife who causes shame is like rottenness in his bones." By shame, it means "to pale" not his face, but his feelings of masculinity and personhood. This may be unseen by you and unspoken by him, but repeated offenses can take a toll on your marriage. I'm certain as a wife you would rather be viewed as a crown and not a clown or cancer to your husband. Your respect or informed sense of awe regarding him brings a crown (reward) to your husband and you because he sees you as a woman who's noble in character. Respect or rottenness, you get to choose. Sista, believe me when I say that your respect is crucial to that Black or non-Black man you will or have married.

Belief #2: Sista, you must believe your role in marriage will be praised (valued) by your children, husband, works (efforts), and God. You can expect that your role will be challenging, challenged, change-making, perhaps changed in some ways, yet weighty in worthiness. When you relate to and respond in proper ways to your role, particularly with respect to your husband's needs, here is a promise you can believe and receive. Proverbs 31:28-30 reads, *"her children rise up and call her blessed; her husband also praises her*: Many women have done noble deeds, but you surpass them all! Charm is deceptive and beauty is fleeting, but a woman who fears *the Lord will be praised.'* Give her the reward of her labor, and *let her works praise her* at the city gates." This praise is not for the average, everyday woman but for you, Sista, as a God-fearing wife.

Belief #3: Sista, you must believe Black marital love grounded in biblical love can make it in marriage, as our ancestors' did. Marital love is made supernatural under God's hand. It's a blend of spiritual, companionate, eros (romantic), sexual, emotional, mental, actional, dedicated, and unconditional agape love. The greatest expression of agape love is Jesus Christ. The greatest explanation of this love is found in 1 Corinthians 13:4-8 where it says, "love is patient, love is kind. Love does not envy, is not boastful, is not arrogant, is not rude, is not self-seeking, is not irritable, and does not keep a record of wrongs. Love finds no joy in unrighteousness but rejoices in the truth. It bears all things, believes all things, hopes all things, and endures all things." This love bears, believes, and behaves in enduring ways.

Belief #4: Sista, you must <u>not</u> believe your husband's mess or mistakes, even his unique Afrocentric issues, cannot be positively influenced by your behavior (actions). Husbands, like everyone else, are mistake prone. They can make a mess of things. Moreover, unlike single men, given the scale of his role and responsibilities and added Afrocentric challenges for the Black male that he is, Sista, the chances increase exponentially for failure on his part. These messes, mistakes, or outright sinful behavior, whether intended or unintended, can range from the trivial to the titanic. But you have a key that may help him reverse course: *your behavior*. Not your beauty. Behavior influences behavior. And this is certainly true in the marriage arena. The Lord promises you as a wife in 1 Peter 3:1-2, "in the same way, wives, submit yourselves to your own husbands so that, even if some disobey the word of God, they may be won over without a word by the way their wives live (behave, carry out your role) when they (husband) observe your pure, reverent lives." To phrase it another way, as your sometimes hard-headed husband sees your God-honoring and caring behavior… it may help bend him toward his own.

Belief #5: Sista, you must <u>never</u> believe God will not help you act on these beliefs, particularly believing (trusting) Him to help a Sista out in marriage. Why? Because these five beliefs are true, growth-oriented, and pro-intimacy. They each stem and have unfettered support from the Maker of marriage—God. God made you to be a wife. God intends marriage to be honorable. God in Christ is Himself married to a Bride called the church or body of Christ. He has a vested interest in His own marriage and yours. Therefore, He obligates Himself to tether these beliefs, informed by the Word of God, to you so they can translate into behaviors leading to blessings for you and your husband.

No one role is more important than the other. However, I suspect, Sista, that you noticed your Nubian husband's role, as with any Christian husband, bears a greater scope of responsibility than yours as his wife. Why? Simple. God made it that way. Your husband is to lead in marriage by loving you the way Christ loves all: *sacrificially*. Of course, you'll find you need to sacrifice at times. But your husband is commanded by God Himself to never abdicate his leading, sacrificial role with you and the kids. Nor are you given consent by God to abdicate your role with your husband and kids.

Chapter 8

Black Men and Women Sharing to Relate The Marriage Option to Their Kids

It's Brighter for Your Kids, Folks

Your marriage should be as favorable to your children as it is to you as spouses. Marriage, particularly in a historically marginalized setting like the Black community, should never be a provocateur of pain and broken promises for your children. Your family unit is to be positively influenced through your married life. As you and your spouse become one "unified whole" as God expects, it will be much easier for you as husband and wife to build a solid and healthy family unit when children are added to the union.

It's not happenstance that the Divine instructions in Ephesians 6 centering on family life follow and serve as a correlated expansion of the Divine instructions governing marital life. After explaining the God-given role and responsibilities of Christian husbands and wives in Ephesians 5:25-33, children's role and responsibilities within the presumed context of marriage are then detailed in Ephesians 6:1-4. "Children, obey your parents in the Lord, because this is right.

Honor your father and mother, which is the first commandment with a promise, so that it may go well with you and that you may have a long life in the land. Fathers, don't stir up anger in your children, but bring them up in the training and instruction of the Lord."

Children are directed here to engage in three crucial disciplines with their parents. They are to (1) *obey their parents,* (2) *honor their parents*, and (3) *permit their parents to bring them up in the training and instruction of the Lord*. Here is the kicker. An indelible connection exists between your spousing and parenting. To be clear, your role as a spouse and parent are not synonymous. But these roles do run side by side. There is some perceived overlap of these two roles in the eyes and experience of children. What this means on a day-to-day basis is (1) Mature spouses tend to make better parents; and (2) to the degree that you consistently, persistently love and respect your spouse and enact your role as we have examined, the easier it will be for your kids to execute their God-given role. When your kids witness repeatedly your positive spousal interactions, it makes obeying and honoring you easier, and permits you as their parents who are spouses to bring them up in the training and instruction of the Lord much easier and with greater chances of success.

To discount this spouse-parent connection is sure to bring outcomes that no child needs or deserves. It results in a marriage that inflicts pain and broken promises which can negatively manifest in minor children and adult offspring in five ways: *Discouragement. Detachment. Deviant behavior. Disparaged future marriage option. Defeatism.*

DISCOURAGEMENT. Brothers and Sistas, do not allow

your good parenting to be negatively affected by poor spousing. If you want to discourage your kid(s), mishandle their "other" parent, who is your spouse in the home. The same is true for single parents but our context here is married life.

The Greek form of the word encouragement means "to comfort, console or calm or even to put in good spirits or mood."[176] The opportunity for the spouse-parent to be a source of encouragement or of discouragement to their children is undeniably present every day. Your kids see your parenting and your spousing. They experience both. They are impacted by both. Of course, they are more directly affected by your parenting. However, I believe kids, are at times directly, indirectly, and instinctively impacted by your spouse relations. And this impact is deeply internalized by them.

Unlike parenting, where kids tend to voice or display their disagreement or excitement for your decisions on the spot, they are less likely to do so when it comes to your spousing. It may be that a child cannot voice or display his or her convictions immediately one way or another because the spousal behavior is hidden. But once the previously hidden negative spousal behavior surfaces, as they tend to do with families living under one roof, and is noticed by the child, it doesn't generally take long for the impact to be felt by a child. And unless you, as the spouse-parent stop the behavior and intervene to help your child process it, the impact will likely come with discouragement for him or her. Please do not permit your spousing to compete with or complicate your parenting. They should complement each other. Ephesians 6:4a urges, "fathers, don't stir up anger in your children." That is, fathers as fathers first and then as spouses, and mothers as mothers first and then as spouses, do not stir up angst in your children.

DETACHMENT. Left unchecked, discouragement mutates into detachment. Through the umbilical cord, a mother and child are attached. Through the sexual procreation act, a husband and wife are attached. Thus, they both are attached anatomy-wise and usually affection-wise from the outset to their child. Children are made in and born for attachment. Detachment from their birth family is particularly traumatizing. Daniel Siegel and Mary Hartzell report that "when children's attachment needs are unmet and their *parent's behavior* is a source of disorientation or terror, they (children) may develop a disorganized attachment. Children with disorganized attachment have repeated experiences of communication in which the parent's behavior is overwhelming, frightening, and chaotic."[177]

It doesn't matter whether the parents' behavior as parents or as spouses cause childhood attachment issues in their young. Either way "attachment research points to the standing of the parent-child relationship in shaping children's interactions with other children, their sense of security about exploring the world, their resilience to stress, their ability to balance their emotions, their capacity to have a coherent story that makes sense of their lives, and their ability to create meaningful *interpersonal relationships in the future (*and present)."[178] A child's detachment from the critical early attachment with mom, dad, and family tends to breed deviant behaviors.

DEVIANT BEHAVIOR. Your spousal behavior has the chance to influence your child's behavior from the crib to the grave. That is, your child, Sista or Brother, might likely behave badly when he or she *repeatedly* witnesses you behaving badly with your spouse, whom they love just as much or more than you do. If your pure and reverent life (behaviors) as a wife, Sista, can help reverse or restore your husband's lack thereof (1 Peter 3:1-2), surely this same behavior can leave a powerful imprint on your child, since kids are so impressionable. And what about fathers acting not only as fathers, but as reverent, upright spouses? It's amazing the behavior cues kids gather from their fathers.

One of our country's most caring, competent, and credible children's advocates, Marian Wright Edelman, pens a powerful letter to parents in *The Sea is So Wide and My Boat is So Small: Charting a Course for the Next Generation*. It's called A Prayer for Twenty-First-Century Children.

> *"God, help us (parents) to not raise a new generation of children with high intellectual quotients and low caring and compassion quotients. With sharp competitive edges but dull cooperative instincts. With highly developed computer skills but poorly developed consciences. With a gigantic commitment to the big I but little sense of responsibility to the bigger we. With mounds of disconnected and un-synthesized information without a moral context to determine its worth. With more and more knowledge and less and less imagination and appreciation for the magic of life that cannot be quantified or computerized. With more and more worldliness and less and less wonder and awe for the sacred and everyday miracles of life. God, help us (parents) to raise children who care."[179]*

Dr. Edelman is advocating that we not raise or contribute to the development of deviant behaviors in our kids. Especially Black kids who are already susceptible to the cradle-to-prison pipeline and other corrosive vices. Brothers and Sistas, beginning with God's Word, long-held Christ-centered values, sound behavioral/psychological science, good ole-fashion common sense, abundant research findings, as well as the spouse-parent witness of our slave and ex-slave ancestors, your spouse-parent role is to provide stimulation, recognition, and certainty (SRC) to your kid(s)—*to the best of your God-given ability*. No kid deserves agitation, rejection, and instability stoked by spouse-parent negligence that leads to deviance in your baby boy or girl. Your spousal and parenting mix should prevent "so many of our children from struggling to cope with family breakdown from pervasive divorce… children suffering from the erosion of extended family and community supports, the loss of civility evidenced by road rage, profane language, and ever coarsening public (and private) discourse so common in our culture. Epidemic substance abuse, domestic violence, and mental illness know no income boundaries."[180]

When our kids suffer from our actions, it should come as no surprise if we find ourselves and others suffering from their actions. Black on Black crime committed by Black youth, drug trafficking, suicide, sexual addiction, emotional disturbance, domestic violence, and other forms of antisocial and criminal behaviors. A special U.S. commission consisting of authorities on child development was convened in the 1990s to examine the general health of adolescents. This report, called *Code Blue,* concluded: "Never before has one generation of American teenagers been less healthy, less cared for, or less prepared for life."[181]

It's no better today, in fact, worse in some ways. Children today, as always, need what our slave and ex-slave relatives were handicapped to grant their offspring, and that is the feeding of their "psychological hunger for Stimulation, Recognition, and Certainty" (SRC).[182] Our black boys and girls in America need SRC in ample supply from spouse-parents to affirm certainty about themselves and life surrounding them. Even when they "rock the boat," our Black girls and boys need to know that they "rock!" and have value.

DISPARAGED FUTURE MARRIAGE OPTION. An even more dire circumstance than deviant behavior is our Black kids struggling to distance themselves from disparaged beliefs about marriage and their own future marriage option.

Marriage is to be "honored or esteemed" by all in it or those engaged to soon be in it, but also by outsiders, even those as young as children as a God-given concept, blessing, and lifestyle (Hebrews 13:4). Children have their convictions about marriage shaped in their formative years. Adam and Eve had their idea and understanding of marriage shaped by God Himself. Since that time, most humans have their beliefs about marriage, and their own marriage option shaped by other humans and their actions or inactions, respect or disdain for, sensitive or sinister handling of, or even a Christ-centered or culture-driven perspective on marriage. Disparaging beliefs about marriage are typically derived from inside the home. Ideally those "insiders in the home" are allowing God in Christ to help shape their children's view of marriage. No wonder the sage in Proverbs 22:6 (KJV) says, "train up a child in the way he should go and when he (she) is old he will not depart from it." Brothers and Sistas, a healthy marriage serve as an excellent training ground for your children's beliefs, hopefully influencing behaviors toward their own good marriage if they choose to marry.

Of course, we know kids sometimes grow up under healthy,

robust spouse-parent marriages and then enter their own marriages and ruin them. The opposite is also true. Kids who grow-up under rocky marriages sometimes occupy their own marital space with booming success. But we are not playing the odds here with kids. The Bible, and much experiential and research evidence, point to the much stronger likelihood of success for kids' future marriage after living under a healthy marriage example. What are some of the disparaging beliefs that can germinate in children who witness a bad marriage?

1) Marriage is a useless relationship to pursue and could not have possibly come from God.

2) Marriage is not worth the personal investment when there exist less sacrificial and painful alternatives like cohabitation (shacking up).

3) I can enjoy all the benefits of marriage without getting married.

4) Heterosexual marriage is not God-ordained, nor is it the only kind of marriage.

5) Marriage does not require hard work to make it successful and wonderful.

6) My first marriage (or as some call it, my "starter" marriage) is practice for my "real" marriage (that is, I will be more "experienced" for my second marriage go round).

7) Marriage as God Himself intended is not to be honored.

Brothers and Sistas, how you and I as Christian-Afrocentric people relate to and relay our roles as spouses has never been more urgent. Because when children harbor such toxic anti-marriage beliefs like these into adulthood, their perspective can go from disparaged beliefs to a feeling of *defeatism* regarding marriage.

DEFEATISM. Imagine your marriage-age child thinking and acting out, I'm of marriage age, but I don't have a winning attitude about marriage. Or I'm dating and deeply in love with a wonderful potential spouse, I even believe God has put us together. But I'm not at all willing to commit or be sacrificial to him or her in marriage because I don't believe it takes all that. If this is your adult son or daughter, he or she may be struggling with defeatism, something worse than "cold feet."

This defeatism might even interfere with them trusting and asking the Lord to help them over this faulty perspective. Or dupe them to forego an appreciation for their Black ancestors as husbands and wives fresh out of slavery, *who knew nothing but forced sacrifice, yet* recognized as a priority and were willing to voluntarily surrender to marriage. Considering the distinguished past record of marriage in the Black experience, any Black person today contemplating, expecting, or hitched in marriage should reflect on why he or she isn't eager to sacrifice for and in marriage with God's help. Because society-wise, church-wise, Christian-wise, man and woman-wise, children-wise, etc., God affirms the benefit of marriage for us all. To be clear, this must not be taken to mean marriage is "for" all. Nevertheless, we need to point out some of the implications of life-long wedlock being better for us all.

It's Better for Us All

In Hebrews 13:4, God said, "marriage is to be honored by all and the marriage bed kept undefiled, because God will judge the sexually immoral and adulterers." Why is marriage better for us all? It's honorable, that is, worth being esteemed or highly valued. As we saw in Genesis 2:18-25, marriage is the original resource used by the Lord God to create on a universal scale human connection leading to family connection. Prior to their arrival in America, our African American ancestors in their native lands enjoyed the human and gender connection marriage made available, like all other cultures around the world. Although their American experience with marriage for the better part of nearly three centuries was a nightmare, this anti-God, anti-American, and anti-African American injustice of marriage didn't fully prevent enslaved or ex-slave Black men and women from deep family connection. The problem was that the connection was in constant threat of abrupt and lasting disconnection at the slave masters' whims in the absence of civil marriage rights. However, for millions of Black people in the South, the legal marriage option secured after the Civil War's end represented what Albert Mohler of Southern Seminary calls the evolution of a "small civilization" within the broader U.S. civilization. Each singular monogamy case is a small civilization of persons necessarily banded together for God-endowed familial purposes.

Marriage still is, and needs to continue to be, as formative for civilization purposes for Blacks, as for any group in our nation. When Black marriages fail (or fail to get off the ground because the couple won't move from engagement to marriage), the people involved not only experience or contribute in some ways to "the death of their own small civilization (marriage/family)," but also to the decline of Black America.

Legal marriage helped Blacks to marshal their precious male and female resources together and fortify both existing families and the new ones to come. It helped them to galvanize an alliance of people, skills, ingenuity, self-determination, imagination, and God-given dreams to erect a new community within the country called the Black community. Stated differently, marriage outcomes in post-Civil War and post-slavery America did what God designed matrimony rights and responsibilities to do for Blacks in the twenty-first century: *provide stability and build, bless, blossom, but never berate a people or Him (Lord God)*. Marriage did that and still does.

Marriage is also honorable and to be esteemed because of its unmatched capacity to protect kids, not just produce them. I coined the term "marriage-carriage" for a preaching event a couple of years ago. The "marriage-carriage" is the natural "in-home" dual protection system every child deserves. I drew the inspiration for the term from Genesis 1:28 when God commanded Adam and Eve "to be fruitful and multiply and fill the earth ..." I think we all can agree it's much easier for spouses in marriage to multiply earth's population through childbirth than to be fruitful in protecting and raising kids once they arrive.

But herein is a protection quagmire for the average Black kid: *out of wedlock birth*. These kids are presently, perhaps permanently, locked out of the positive, profound, and penetrating impact of healthy weddedness. Please hear my heart and head here. If you're a single mother or father, I'm not out to be judgmental because your parenting role is of no less value to the Lord than anyone else's. I'm fully aware a Black child, any child for that matter, is not automatically doomed to be protection-less or to fail because he or she was raised in a single-parent household. I know single parents, like I'm sure you do, whose kids turned out fine, but it was not easy. And many of the unwed black mothers I know would rather be married than having to bear the brunt of the child rearing duty alone. Still, it's no denying odds are stacked against Black kids born out-of-wedlock. What I find dynamic is our ex-slave predecessors went into marriage, birthed, and raised their own kids, and often even brought and raised kids who were not their biological kids into their family to protect them. However, in the last several decades or so, Black America has shown a stubborn penchant for doing the exact opposite.

Over the years, I have often wondered how our two sons, who are now grown and married with kids of their own, would have turned out if my wife and I hadn't resurrected our marriage. I don't know. But I did receive a brief taste of what single parenting is like twenty-six years ago and didn't like what I was seeing, nor what our two kids were experiencing. So may I say if the ideal opportunity presents itself to wed, with the added chance to aid your kids, do it. Get married. Do it as you make it your mantra to commit to the following in marriage: *(1) I will be fruitful and multiply in protecting my kids – Genesis 1:28, (2) I will train up my kids in the way they should go (God's way) – Proverbs 22:6, (3) I will see my kids as an inheritance, thus an investment from the Lord—not just from the other parent – Psalm 127:3-5, (4) I will not intentionally do anything to prohibit my kids from Jesus Christ – Matthew 19:13-15,*

(5) I will not stir my kids to anger or wrath – Ephesians 6:4, (6) I will work to love my kids like God in Christ loves me as His spiritual child – 1 Corinthians 13:4-8, and (7) I will do all I can in God's strength to protect my kids via the marriage-carriage – Matthew 18:1-6, Matthew 19.

One sure-fire way you can protect your kids, yourself, and your nuptials is by keeping sex within your marriage. Marriage offers the safest sexual union of all. The Lord God has a vested interest in your safe-sex practices. He wants your marital sexual intimacy to be fulfilling, fun, and good—but safe, as in sanctifying.

Whether He is your God or not, the fallout from the seeming all-out, no-holds-barred sex campaign in our current generation resonates with God in Christ. And it should resonate with you enough to make you quarantine your sexual activities to marriage. Sex outside of marriage is having detrimental and widespread effects on our marriages today. Veteran counselor and relationship expert, Dr. Lana Staheli, along with other studies, reports that upwards of 60% of marriages are victimized by an affair.[183] In my twenty five-year counseling ministry, primarily with Black couples, extramarital affairs have been consistent among the couples I have tried to help. I can tell you from both personal and professional experience, adulterous sex is not safe sex. In fact, it usually impacts more than sex relations. Trust, family stability, finances, emotional and/or mental and physical equilibrium, spiritual standing, school/work habits, and integrity are just some of the other casualties.

You must work to keep your marriage safe-sex friendly because you cannot expect our overly sexualized culture to coddle your marriage. Yet, your guardianship is exponentially more challenging than our ancestors' was due to 1) technology placing sexual alternative practices at any and everyone's fingertips, and 2) a mutation from the sexual revolution of the 60s to a sexual evolution of the twenty-first century. Society is no longer just interested in how much and with whom we have sex, but in how much sex can be perverted from its original God-given and God-honored aims. Only you, as an individual in marriage can guard yourself, your spouse, marriage, family, reputation, and body from this sexual evolution age and its invasion. In doing so you will also guard yourself from the judgment of someone greater: God.

God frowns on affairs (adultery). Turning again to scripture, Hebrews 13:4 says, "marriage is to be honored by all and the marriage bed kept undefiled, because God will judge the sexually immoral and adulterers (the affairee)." Proverbs 6:32 says, "one who commits *adultery* lacks sense and destroys himself." In Mt. 5:27-28, Jesus Himself said, "you have heard that it was said, do not commit *adultery*. But I tell you, everyone who looks at a woman lustfully has already committed *adultery* with her in his heart." Note that the scriptures advocate for your safe sex practices not by promoting use of a condom, or some pill, or uterine device (although I would urge their use if you, your spouse, or any single person are bent on violating God's dictates). The fleeting pleasure in adultery will, in time, turn into nothing more than sex headed for a wreck in the marriage-carriage. It has the potential to wreak havoc on the relationship. On the flip side, the more you work to build up, maintain, and protect your marriage from unauthorized sex and God's judgment, the more you'll be helping to blossom the community that is within your current or future small civilization we refer to as a monogamous marriage and family.

When marriages or the idea of marriage as a concept disintegrates, the uplift of the community automatically downshifts. A real story is told of a husband, wife, and small family—small civilization—that disintegrated. As this Black marriage fell apart, moving from brokenness to separation and eventual divorce, the neighbors noticed how frequently the driveway's watch light was left burning overnight. Previously the watch light was turned off at a designated time in late evening. But when the security of the nuptials was compromised, leading to separation and divorce, the community or neighborhood felt the ripple effect. How was that you ask? The husband was no longer present. The strong couple was no longer a reality. Thus, those remaining in the home, the wife and kids, felt less safe. Sadly, this ground-zero breach reverberates in hearts, homes, and neighborhoods across the nation. I pray not yours!

This completes our review of your respective roles as husband and wife. Both of you have enormous, and what may sometimes feel like enigmatic, roles. But when they are embraced, they are expressive, energizing, and enriching to your marriage life. To the Black community. To community, in general.

Chapter 9

Conclusion

Blacks today increasingly need hope, help, and healing to keep their marriage option alive and well. Not just individually or as a couple, but also collectively as a people. Regrettably, as it stands in 2022, the statistics and overall situation on marriage are worse across the main three ethnic groups in the U.S., it is especially troubling for Black America. Getting married, staying married, or respect for marriage are hopeless situations in the hearts and minds of many Blacks. Is there hope? Can we progress beyond this point and reach a more stable and sustainable position on marriage that will glorify God, the Maker of marriage? I think so. I hope so. I want it to be so.

But this venture toward progress will take struggle, just as it did with our ancestors. The Black church needs to be at the forefront of this effort, as it once was, serving to destigmatize marriage and its distorted meaning and practice in the hearts and minds of many Blacks. I'm not suggesting that the Black church abandon the proclamation of the gospel and its kingdom agenda as its central aim. The church must never do that. But I am saying, as a part of its kingdom agenda, marriage and its corollary, family, must run a close second because they are a strong focus in God's kingdom agenda.

Aside from the church, marriage help can also be found in clergy, counseling, and concentrated small group support. However, these resources can only do so much. God in Christ will, for certain, do His part. Counselors or small groups can offer their skilled and caring aid. But how you, Sista or Brother, represent your role in marriage is central to making matrimony work.

I remember making a personal vow in the mid-nineties when my marriage was in trouble. At that time, my wife and I were physically separated by hundreds of miles. Our separation also kept me apart from our two little boys. After having undergone a spiritual renewal somewhat like the prodigal dude in Luke 15, I vowed unto God that since I didn't handle my sons' mom and our marriage right, I was going to do all I could to reverse course. Thankfully, by the amazing grace and help of the Lord Jesus, we didn't lose the marriage. With His guidance, coupled with our own hard work, persistence, and patience, we recovered and healed and are stronger than ever—by far. Even after all these years, it still brings tears to my eyes when I think of God's faithfulness to me—especially, my wife, and to our small civilization called the Walker family.

But one defining occurrence took place for my wife and me that was essential to our comeback as a Black married couple. We both began to seize on the God-given opportunity to truly exemplify to each other and our kids our distinct responsibility in marriage. My wife BJ and I discussed at length and began to grasp and grow in the unique spiritual, biblical, relational, and behavioral position of spouses. Each role makes marriage brighter for your kids. And clear interpersonal identity makes marriage better universally for all in

Black America, and the U.S. population in general. No marriage by Blacks, Whites, or whoever can happen, much less heal and head-off in the right direction without this personalized realization and execution of spousal duty.

We don't have to, nor should we be, living out a "post-marriage" culture. The cost in so many ways is too great and spiritually negligible to do so. I enlist your help and resilience to resist contributing to a post-marriage culture for America, Black America, or yourself and family. The progress, stability, and hope for a turnaround we have explored in this book rest not in a new formula. It lies in using the foundational and formative blueprint our ancestors were given by God and used to secure and sustain marriage: *Christ, Church, Character, and Civil discourse.* All the other resources like counseling, concentrated small group, etc., are added but necessary firepower you can bring to the fight to help salvage our Black marriage option. All in Jesus name. Amen.

About The Author

Rev. Dr. Roosevelt Walker, Sr., has served for nearly twenty years as Senior Pastor of the Faith United Missionary Baptist Church in Nashville, Tennessee. For twenty-five years he has been a sought-after pastoral caregiver on marriage. A board-certified pastoral counselor (BCPC) with the American Association of Christian Counselors (AACC), Dr. Walker holds degrees in business, theology, and a D.MIN. degree in Formational Counseling from Ashland Theological Seminary. He and his wife, Benita, have been married since 1988 and have two married adult sons and three beautiful grandkids.

Also by Rev. Dr. Roosevelt Walker, Sr.

Beginning at birth, each of us is continually thrust into matters of life-changing importance. *Lifetime Matters* is a Bible-based devotional in which Dr. Walker highlights issues, inclinations, and God-given inspirations pertaining to Lifetime Matters like: the meaning of life; family; God's will; daily matters we all face; the birth of Jesus Christ (and our rebirth); your emotions; your mentality (or as Dr. Walker likes to say, "your mentals,"); passion for people; and church life. If you feel that your life doesn't matter or doesn't matter enough, the Christ-informed insights in this book will help.

Endnotes

1   Nancy Boyd-Franklin, Black Families in Therapy: A Multi-systems Approach (New York: Guilford Press, 1989), p. 222.

2   Nancy Boyd-Franklin, Black Families in Therapy, 222.

3   Joyce Hansen, Bury Me Not in A Land of Slaves: African American in the Time of Reconstruction (New York: Grolier Publishing, 2000), 57.

4   Betty Stroud, The Reconstruction Era (New York: Marshall Covendish Benchmark, 2007), 35-36.

5   Henry Lewis Gates, Jr., Dark Sky Rising: Reconstruction and the Dawn of Jim Crow (New York: Scholastic Focus, 2019), p. 51-52.

6   Nora Lee Frankel, Break Those Chains at Last: African Americans 1860-1880 (New York: Oxford University Press, 1996), 43.

7   C. Eric Lincoln and Lawrence H. Mamiya. The Black Church in African the American Experience (Durham, NC: Duke University Press, 1990), 8.

8   Norma Jean Lutz, The History of the Black Church (Philadelphia, PA: Chelsea House Publishers, 2001), 26-27.

9   Nora Lee Frankel, Break Those Chains at Last, 102.

10   Stephen Currie, Life of A Slave on A Southern Plantation (San Diego, CA: Lucent Books, 2000), 65.

11   E. Franklin Frazier, The Negro Church in America (New York: Schocken Books, 1964), 38.

12   Nora Lee Frankel, Break Those Chains at Last, 102.

13   Nora Lee Frankel, Break Those Chains at Last, 102.

14   U. S. Census Bureau, "Number, Timing, and Duration of Marriages and Divorces: 2009." Current Population Reports, P70-125, 24, Washington, DC, 2011.

15   Paul Escott, Slavery Remembered: A Record of Twentieth-Century Slave Narratives (Chapel Hill, NC: University of North Carolina Press, 1979), 169.

16   Bryant, Chandra M. Understanding the intersection of race and marriage: does one model fit all http://www.apa.org/science/about/psa/2010/10/race marriage.aspx (accessed September 2012), 3.

17   Ralph Richard Banks, Is Marriage for White People? (New York, NY: Peguin, 2011), 8.

18   Anne M. Halley, Developmental Formational Prayer (Ohio, 2009), 10.

19   Anne M. Halley, Developmental Formational Prayer, 10.

20   Chandra M. Bryant, Understanding the intersection of race and marriage, 3.

21   Chandra M. Bryant, Understanding the intersection of race and marriage: does one model fit all, 4.

22   Robert Staples, An Overview of Race and Marital Status. In Black Families, ed. Harriette P. McAdoo (Thousand Oaks, CA: Sage Publications, 1997), 269.

23   Audrey B. Chapman, The Black Search for Love and Devotion. In Black Families, ed. Harriette P. McAdoo (Thousand Oaks, CA: Sage Publications, 1997), 273-274.

24   Audrey B. Chapman, Entitled to Good Loving: Black Men and Women and The Battle for Love and Power (New York: Henry Holt and Company, 1995), 4.

25   Audrey B. Chapman, Entitled to Good Loving, 22.

26   David A. Seamands, Healing from Damaged Emotions (Wheaton, IL: Victor Books, 1991), 33.

27   Audrey B. Chapman, The Black Search for Love and Devotion, 277.

28   Reggie McNeal, Practicing Greatness (San Francisco, CA: Jossey-Bass, 2006), 22.

29   Terry Wardle, Healing Care, Healing Prayer (Abilene, TX: Leafwood Publishers, 2001), 136-137.

30   Nancy Boyd-Franklin, Black Families in Therapy, 10.

31   Stephen Seamands, Wounds That Heal (Downers Grove, IL: InterVarsity, 2003), 29.

32   Leanne Payne, Restoring the Christian Soul (Grand Rapids, MI: Baker Group, 1996), 36.

33   Stephen Seamans, Wounds That Heal, 31-35.

34   Orlando Patterson, Rituals of Blood: Consequences of Slavery in Two American Centuries (Washington D.C.: Civitas Counterpoint, 1998), 160-167.

35   Ken R. Canfield, The 7 Secrets of Effective Fathers (Whea-

ton, IL: Tyndale House, 1992), 34.

36   Ken R. Canfield, The 7 Secrets of Effective Fathers, 35-36.

37   Brenda Richardson and Brenda Wade, What Mama Couldn't Tell Us About Love (New York: Harper Collins, 1999), 93-94.

38   Don S. Browning, Marriage and Modernization: How Globalization Threatens Marriage and What to Do About It (Grand Rapids, MI: Eerdsman Publishing, 2003), 79.

39   Ralph Richardson Banks, Is Marriage for White People? 29.

40   Michelle Alexander, The New Jim Crow (New York: New Press, 2012), 60,100.

41   Ralph Richardson Banks, Is Marriage for White People, 31.

42   S. Hatchett, E. Douvan and J. Veroff, Marital Instability: A Social and Behavioral Study of the Early Years (Westport, CT: Praeger Publishers, 1995), p. xiii.

43   Claudia Pinto, "Marriage Eludes Many Black Women," The Tennessean, November 7, 2010.

44   Brenda Richardson and Brenda Wade, What Mama Couldn't Tell Us About Love, 22-24.

45   Brenda Richardson and Brenda Wade, What Mama Couldn't Tell Us About Love, 14-22.

46   Shaunti and Jeff Feldhahn, For Men Only (Atlanta, GA: Multnomah, 2006), 27.

47   Brenda Richardson and Brenda Wade, What Mama Couldn't Tell Us About Love, 17.

48   Ralph Richardson Banks, Is Marriage for White People? 33.

49   Ralph Richardson Banks, Is Marriage for White People? 68-71.

50   H. P. McAdoo, Black Families (Thousand Oaks, CA: Sage Publications, 1997), 36.

51   Jesse Washington, "Debate Flares Over Unwed Black Mothers," The Tennessean, November 7, 2010.

52   Brenda Richardson and Brenda Wade, What Mama Couldn't Tell Us About Love, 86.

53   Ralph Richardson Banks, Is Marriage for White People? 7.

54   Ralph Richardson Banks, Is Marriage for White People? 7-10.

55   Mary Hartzell and Daniel Seigel, Parenting from the Inside Out (New York: Peguin, 2003), 122-123.

56   Nancy Boyd-Franklin, Black Families in Therapy, 221.

57   Brenda Richardson and Brenda Wade, What Mama Couldn't Tell Us About Love, 5-6.

58   Mary Hartzell and Daniel Seigel, Parenting from the Inside Out, 21-28.

59   Reggie McNeal, Practicing Greatness, 10-11.

60   Nancy Boyd-Franklin, Black Families in Therapy, 225-227.

61   Mary Hartzell and Daniel Seigel, Parenting from the Inside Out, 60, 101.

62   Anne M. Halley, Developmental Formational Prayer, 27.

63   Anne M. Halley, Developmental Formational Prayer, 30.

64   Mary Hartzell and Daniel Seigel, Parenting from the Inside Out, 1-2.

65   William T. Kirwan, Biblical Concepts for Christian Counseling (Grand Rapids, MI: Baker Publishing, 1984), 42-56.

66   Reggie McNeal, Practicing Greatness, 19-21.

67   T.D. Jakes, Loose That Man and Let Him Go (Tulsa, OK: Albury Press, 1995), 9.

68   Nancy Boyd-Franklin, Black Families in Therapy, 222.

69   Howard Clinebell, Basic Types of Pastoral Care and Counseling (Nashville, TN: Abingdon Press, 1984), 190-197.

70   Douglas McMurry and Everett Worthington, Marriage Conflicts (Grand Rapids, MI: Baker Group, 1994), 32.

71   Kumea Shorter-Gooden and Charisse Jones, Shifting: The Double Lives of Black Women in America (New York: HarperCollins Publishers, 2003), 139.

72   Harold Koenig, Faith and Mental Health (West Conshohocken, TN: Templeton Foundation Press, 2005), 173-174, 177.

73   Douglas McMurry and Everett Worthington, Marriage Conflicts, 32.

74   Norma Jean Lutz, The History of the Black Church (Philadelphia, PA: Chelsea House Publishers, 2001), 9-11.

75   Albert J. Raboteau, Slave Religion, 212.

76   E. Franklin Frazier, The Negro Church in America, (New York: Schocken Books, 1963), 45.

77   E. Franklin Frazier, The Negro Church in America, 29-31, 44-46.

78   Edward L. Wheeler, Uplifting the Race: The Black Minister in the New South 1865-1902 (Lanham, MD: University Press of America, 1986), 17-30.

79   Leon F. Litwack, Trouble in Mind: Black Southerners in the Age of Jim Crow (New York: Random House, 1998), 380.

80   Harold Koenig, Faith and Mental Health, 170-172.

81   Irvin D. Yalom, The Theory and Practice of Group Psychotherapy (New York: Basic Books Publisher, 1970), 215.

82   Irvin D. Yalom, The Theory and Practice of Psychotherapy, 5

83   Howard Clinebell, Basic Types of Pastoral Care and Counseling (Nashville, TN: Abingdon Press, 1984), 349-352.

84   Donna Thomas, The Healing Christ in Community (Ashland, OH: Rose Publishers, 2009), 4-7.

85   Donna Thomas, The Healing Christ in Community, 8.

86   Julie A. Gorman, Community That is Christian (Grand Rapids, MI: Baker Books, 2002), 11, 94-96.

87   Janice M. Rasheed and Mikal N. Rasheed, Social Work Practice with African American Men, 106.

88   Ay Ling Jan and Melba J.T. Vasquez, "Group Interventions and Treatment with Ethnic Minorities," In Psychological Interventions and Cultural Diversity, eds. Joseph F. Aponte, Robin Young Rivers, Julian Wohl (Needham Heights, MA: Ally and Bacon, 1955), 111-113.

89   William T. Kirwan, Biblical Concepts for Christian Counseling, 21.

90   Charles Kraft, Confronting Powerless Christianity (Grand Rapids, MI: Baker Publishing, 2002), 133.

91   Terry Wardle, Healing Care, Healing Prayer (Abilene, TX: Leafwood Publishers, 2001), 86.

92   Terry Wardle, Healing Care, Healing Prayer, 190.

93   Gerald May, Care of Mind Care of Spirit, 2.

94   Terry Wardle, Wounded: How to Find Wholeness and Inner Healing in Christ (Abilene, TX: Leafwood Publishers, 1994, 2005), 146-147.

95   Donna Thomas, The Healing Community in Christ, 6.

96   Henry Cloud and John Townsend, How People Grow (Grand Rapids, MI: Zondervan, 2001), 81.

97   Donna Thomas, The Healing Christ in Community, 15.

98   Howard Clinebell, Basic Types of Pastoral Care and Counseling, 352.

99   Donna Thomas, The Healing Christ in Community, 50.

100   Terry Wardle, Healing Care, Healing Prayer, 86.

101   Henry Cloud and John Townsend, How People Grow, 81.

102   Terry Wardle, Healing Care, Healing Prayer, 95.

103   Henry Cloud and John Townsend, How People Grow, 81.

104   Greg Boyd, Present Perfect: Finding God in the Now (Grand Rapids: MI: Zondervan, 2010), 10, 15.

105   James Bryan Smith, The Good and Beautiful God (Downers Grove, IL: InterVarsity, 2009), 40.

106   J. Brent Bill and Beth A. Booram, Awaken Your Senses (Downers Grove, IL: InterVarsity Press, 2012), 18.

107   Larry Crabb, Connecting (Nashville, TN: Thomas Nelson, 1997), 31.

108   Mary Gordon, Roots of Empathy (New York: The Experiment Publishing, 2009), 62.

109   Howard Clinebell, Basic Types of Pastoral Care and Counseling, 257.

110   William T. Kirwan, Biblical Concepts for Christian Counseling, 176-177.

111   Mary Hartzell and Daniel Siegel, Parenting from the Inside Out, 7.

112   Henry Cloud and John Townsend, How People Grow, 81.

113   Jean Clarke and Connie Dawson, Growing Up Again (Center City, MN: Hazelden, 1998), 149-155.

114   Myles Munroe, Understanding the Purpose and Power of Prayer (New Kensington, PA: Whitaker House, 2002), 7-8.

115   University of Michigan study, Blacks Use Prayer to Cope with Stress. *http://ns.umich.edu/new/release/6504*. April 23, 2008 interne article.

116   Terry Wardle, Strong Winds and Crashing Waves (Abilene, TX: Leafwood Publishers, 2007), 18-19.

117   Brenda Richardson and Brenda Wade, What Mama Couldn't Tell Us About Love,135.

118   Brenda Richardson and Brenda Wade, What Mama Couldn't Tell Us About Love, 3.

119   J. Daniel Hays, From Every People and Nation: A Biblical Theology of Race (Downer's Grove, IL: InterVarsity Press, 2003), 45, 31.

120   Renita J. Weems, What Matters Most: Ten Lessons in Living Passionately from the Song of Solomon (New York: Warner Books, 2004), 32.

121   Robert W. Jenson, Songs of Songs Interpretation Louisville, KY: John Knox Press, 2005), 50.

122   Neil T. Anderson and Charles Mylander, The Christ Centered Marriage: Discovering and Enjoying Your Freedom in Christ (Venture, CA: Regal Books, 1996), 56.

123   Daniel Akin, God on Sex: The Creator's Idea About Love, Intimacy, and Marriage (Nashville, TN: Broadman and Holman, 2003), 13.

124   Theophile J. Meek, The Song of Songs. In the Interpreter's Bible, ed. George A. Buttrick (Nashville: Abingdon, 1965), 143.

125   James Strong, The Exhaustive Concordance of the Bible (Nashville: Holman Bible Publishers).

126   J. Cheryl Exum, Songs of Songs (Louisville, KY: Westminster John Knox Press, 2005), 241.

127   Theophile J. Meek, The Song of Songs. In the Interpreter's Bible, ed. George A. Buttrick, 139.

128   Robert C. Dentan, The Song of Songs. In the Interpreter's One-Volume Commentary of the Bible, ed. Charles M. Laymon (Nashville: Abingdon, 1971), 327.

129   Hugh T. Kerr and Hugh T. Kerr, Jr., The Song of Songs. In the Interpreter's Bible, ed. George A. Buttrick (Nashville: Abingdon, 1956), 138.

130   J. Cheryl Exum, Songs of Songs, 209.

131   Richard Hess, Baker Commentary on the Old Testament, 188.

132   Sierd, Woudstra, The Song of Songs. The Wycliffe Bible Commentary, ed. Charles P. Pfeiffer (Nashville: The Southwestern

Company, 1962), 601.

133   Robert C. Dentan, The Proverbs. In the Interpreter's One-Volume Commentary of the Bible, ed. Charles M. Laymon (Nashville: Abingdon, 1971), 319.

134   Milton P. Horne, Proverbs-Ecclesiastes (Macon, GA: Smith and Helwys Publishing, 2003), 364.

135   Leo G. Perdue, Proverbs: A Bible Commentary for Teaching and Preaching (Louisville, KY: John Knox Press, 2000), 280.

136   Robert Dentan, The Proverbs. In the Interpreter's One-Volume Commentary of the Bible, ed. Charles M. Laymon, 319.

137   Milton P. Horne, Proverbs-Ecclesiastes, 360.

138   James Strong, The Exhaustive Concordance of the Bible (Nashville: Holman Bible Publishers).

139   Renita J. Weems, Battered Love: Marriage, Sex, and Violence in the Hebrew Prophets (Minneapolis, MN: Augsburg Fortress, 1995), 114.

140   Knox Chamblin, Matthew: A Mentor Commentary. Vol. 2, 926.

141   E. G. Gould, International Critical Commentary (New York: Charles Scribner's Sons, 1905), 184.

142   Rudolph Bultmann, Theology of the New Testament (New York: Charles Scribner's Sons, 1955), 15.

143   Homer A. Kent, Jr., The Gospel According to Matthew. The Wycliffe Bible Commentary, ed. Everett F. Harrison (Nashville: The Southwestern Company, 1962), 963.

144   Philip Roderick, Beloved: Henri Nouwen in Conversation (Grand Rapids, MI: Eerdmans Publishing, 2007), 6.

145   Colin Gunton, The Promise of the Trinity (Edinburgh: T & T Clark, 1991), 116.

146   Howard Thurman, Jesus and The Disinherited (Boston: Beacon Press, 1976), 9-10.

147   Henri Nouwen, The Road to Peace (Maryknoll, NY: Orbis Books, 1988), 202.

148   Edmond Jacob, Theology of the Old Testament (New York: Harper and Row, 1958), 172.

149   Edmond Jacob, Theology of the Old Testament, 172.

150   Michael Spencer, Mere Churchianity (Colorado Springs,

CO: Waterbrook Press, 2010), 178-179.

151   Terry Wardle, Draw Close to the Fire (Abilene, TX: Leaf-wood Publishing, 2004), 148.

152   Michael Spencer, Mere Churchianity, 182.

153   Philip Roderick, Beloved: Henri Nouwen in Conversation, 8, 15.

154   Michael Spencer, Mere Churchianity, 182.

155   James H. Cone, A Black Theology of Liberation (Philadelphia: Lippincott, 1970), 11.

156   Bruce L. Fields, Introducing Black Theology: 3 Crucial Questions for the Evangelical Church, 74.

157   Bruce L. Fields, Introducing Black Theology: 3 Crucial Questions for the Evangelical Church, 74-75.

158   Anthony B. Bradley, Liberating Black Theology, 179-180.

159   Anthony B. Bradley, Liberating Black Theology, 180-191.

160   Renita J. Weems, What Matters Most: Ten Lessons in Living Passionately from the Song of Solomon (New York: Warner Books, 2004).

161   James Childerston, "Beyond Chemistry: Understanding the Neurobiology of Sex," Christian Counseling Today 21, no. 1, 12.

162   James Strong, The Exhaustive Concordance of the Bible (Nashville: Holman Bible Publishers).

163   James Strong, The Exhaustive Concordance of the Bible (Nashville: Holman Bible Publishers).

164   Tim Keller, The Reason for God: Belief in an Age of Skepticism (New York: Penguin Group, 2008), 48.

165   Tim Keller, The Reason for God: Belief in an Age of Skepticism, 50.

166   Emerson Eggerichs, Love and Respect (Brentwood, TN: Integrity Publishers, 2004), 183-249.

167   Emerson Eggerichs, Love and Respect, 117-173.

168   Shaunti Feldhahn, For Women Only (Atlanta, GA: Multnomah Publishers, 2004), 21-53.

169   James Strong, The Exhaustive Concordance of the Bible (Nashville: Holman Bible Publishers).

170   Gary Chapman, The Five Love Languages (Chicago, IL: Northfield Publishing, 1995), 165-166.

171   Gary Chapman, The Five Love Languages, 16-17.

172   See "Myriad Opportunities in Ethnic Merchandising," Business and Industry, February 25, 2002, 19(4): 28, and "BeautyandSoul.com Finally Answers Needs of Largest Beauty Consumer—Black Women," PR Newswire, November 16, 1999.

173   Kumea Shorter-Gooden and Charisse Jones, Shifting: The Double Lives of Black Women in America, 177.

174   Darlene Clark Hine and Kathleen Thompson, A Shining Thread of Hope: The History of Black Women in America (New York: Broadway Books, 1998),

175   Kumea Shorter-Gooden and Charisse Jones, Shifting: The Double Lives of Black Women in America, 124.

176   James Strong, The Exhaustive Concordance of the Bible (Nashville: Holman Bible Publishers).

177   Mary Hartzell and Daniel Siegel, Parenting from the Inside Out, 105.

178   Mary Hartzell and Daniel Siegel, Parenting from the Inside Out, 101-105.

179   Marian Wright Edelman, The Sea is So Wide and My Boat is so Small: Charting a Course for the Next Generation (New York: Hyperion Books, 2008), 1.

180   Marian Wright Edelman, The Sea is so Wide and My Boat is so Small: Charting a Course for the Next Generation, 4.

181   Warren Leary, "Gloomy Report on the Health of Teenagers," New York Times, June 9, 1990, 24.

182   Jean Clarke and Connie Dawson, Growing Up Again (Center City, MN: Hazelden, 1998), 13-14.

183   Lana Staheli, Affair Proof Your Marriage: Understanding, Preventing and Surviving an Affair (New York: Harper Perennial, 1998), 9.